THE COMMUNITY
OF LIVING THINGS

FIELD and
MEADOW

THE COMMUNITY OF LIVING THINGS

in

FIELD AND MEADOW

BY

ETTA SCHNEIDER RESS, Ed.D.

in co-operation with

THE NATIONAL AUDUBON SOCIETY

NEW YORK CITY

CREATIVE EDUCATIONAL SOCIETY, Inc.

MANKATO, MINNESOTA

FOREWORD

Adam and Eve, we are told, were banished from the Garden of Eden because they broke the law their master had laid down. Instead of living in a bountiful garden where life was right and beautiful, they were forced to scramble for a living in a harsh land.

Ever since, Adam's children have found that life became harder if they broke the laws of nature. Primitive man found that they would perish if they ignored these basic rules. Today, some men seem to regard themselves as beings apart from, not a part of, nature. They place mankind in one category, the rest of the world in another. But we know how dangerous this thinking is. True, man is the most adaptable animal in the world; his kind thrives on every continent, and in nearly every environment, from the humid tropics to the polar regions, from the sea's edge to high mountains. But one universal rule he must follow: to survive he must live in harmony with his environment.

The study of the relation of living things to their environment is called *ecology*. This way of studying animals, plants, and human beings considers the *whole* rather than its separate parts. That does not mean that the parts are not important; for one cannot have a house without bricks, stones, or pieces of wood. But it is the way the parts fit together that make the finished structure.

This book, the first in a series dealing with the COMMUNITY OF LIVING THINGS, concerns itself with the fields and meadows — grass, humble but important. Pictures, which do many things that words cannot, are used profusely to tell this story.

Grass is the great wall of defense between civilization and the desert. Grasslands feed men while deserts offer a scrawny living. The best buffer against erosion, the wearing away of the soil, is a healthy sod. Birds, mammals, insects, and other wildlife are as much a part of a meadow as the grass itself. But I am anticipating the contents of this book; all this, and what it means to mankind, is told very clearly by Dr. Ress and her associates, and by the carefully chosen photographs.

Roger Tory Peterson

CONTENTS

Foreword 7
Preface 9

CHAPTER I — LIFE IN THE FIELD COMMUNITY

The Field is More Than
    What we See 11
Above it are Air and Sunlight 12
Below it is Soil 14
Plants and Animals Live There 16

Spring in the Fields 17
Summer in the Fields 18
Autumn in the Fields 19
Winter in the Fields 20

CHAPTER II — PLANTS THAT LIVE IN THE FIELD

An Introduction to Plants 23
Plants that Man Puts to Work 24
Mushrooms, Plants without
    Chlorophyll 26
Some Flowers Need Insects 27
Wildflowers of the Field: Daisies .. 28
Pods Bursting in Air 30

"Leaflets Three, Let it Be" 31
Cultivated and Uncultivated
    Grasses 32
Cereal Plants 34
Shrubs of the Fields 36
In the Shade of the
    Old Apple Tree 37

CHAPTER III — COLD BLOODED ANIMALS OF THE FIELD

The Grasshopper 40
The Praying Mantis
    Hunts His Prey 41
Insects We can Hear: The
    Katydid and the Grasshopper 42
The Ground Cricket 43
The Common Cicada 44
Aphids, Insect "Cows" 45
Beetles 46
The Monarch Butterfly:
    Egg and Larva 47
From Caterpillar to Chrysalis 48
Hail to the Monarch 49
The Monarch Butterfly,
    Winter Migrant 50

The Black Swallowtail Butterfly .. 51
The Sphinx Moth 52
Ants 53
Bumblebees 54
The Honeybee 55
An Apiary 56
The Paper-making wasp 57
The Earthworm, Plowman
    of the Earth 58
The Orange Garden Spider 59
Toads 60
The Box Turtle 61
Snakes of the Field 62
A New Generation of Snakes 63

CHAPTER IV — BIRDS: WARM-BLOODED ANIMALS WITH FEATHERS

Birds are Streamlined for Flight 65
How Birds Fly 66
Birds, Our Fine-feathered
    Friends 67
Where Are the Birds in Winter? 68
Overwintering Birds 70
Birds that Live in the Fields:
    The Meadowlark 72
The Sparrows 73
The Barn Swallow 74
The Bluebird 75

The Eastern Kingbird 76
The Killdeer 77
Gamebirds of the Field:
    The Bob-white Quail 78
The Ring-necked Pheasant 79
A Mother Pheasant
    and her Brood 80
Birds of Prey: Hawks 81
Owls 82
Sanitation Crew of the Fields 83

CHAPTER V — MAMMALS: WARM-BLOODED ANIMALS WITH HAIR

Feeding Time for Meadow Mice 85
The Thirteen Lined
    Ground Squirrel 86
The Woodchuck 87
The Pocket Gopher:
    An Underground Worker 88
The Cottontail Rabbit 89
The Jack Rabbit 90

Roundup Time on the Range 91
The Skunk, a Plant-eater
    and a Flesh-eater 92
The Badger, a Burrowing
    Flesh-eater 93
The Coyote, Prairie Wolf 94
The Red Fox 95

CHAPTER VI — THE COMMUNITY OF LIVING THINGS

A Field Community 97
Fields in Balance 98
A Field out of Balance 100
Gullies Where Crops Once Grew 102
A Patchwork of Fertile Fields 104
The Rotation of Crops 106
Man Against Insects 108
"Grass Once Grew There, Too" 110
The Cattle of Yesteryear 112

A Haven for Wildlife 114
The Hunting Season is on 115
Young Workers for Wildlife 116
From Knowledge comes Pleasure .. 118
Watching for Wildlife 119

Index 121
Picture Acknowledgments 124

PREFACE

THIS IS A PICTURE-STORY of the plants and animals that live in open spaces and how they live together in a community. We have not included *all* the species that live in *all* the fields, but we have tried to show typical ones.

By fields are meant the areas that are non-forested and uncultivated, where weeds, grasses, and wildlife live in a natural state; also the open spaces in cultivated grain or vegetable fields, meadows where hay crops flourish, and pastures where cows or sheep graze.

In this book you are being introduced to your own field communities.

The pictures and brief texts will help you explore these sunny places, discover some of their interesting inhabitants and see how they manage to withstand the continuous sunlight and often intense heat of a summer day, the drying winds, the long periods of winter cold.

CHAPTER I

Life in the Field Community

The Field Is More Than What We See

Here is a field. Besides the many plants you see, there are animals in great numbers — multitudes of insects and spiders; earthworms and hosts of other small creatures are in the ground. Feeding on seeds are sparrows and other seed-eaters. Mice, rabbits, and woodchucks also feed on plants. Insects devour quantities of plants. The insects provide food for birds, shrews, skunks, and for many others.

A field can support only a limited population of plants and animals. When there are too many of one kind, some must die for lack of food, space, shelter, and nesting places. Some must provide food for others.

Certain plants and animals can live only in a field. In the long space of time they have lived they have become adjusted to life in open spaces. They can withstand the dryness and heat of summer in the open field, the winds and cold of winter. They can manage with little water. Many plants and animals of the field would perish if transplanted to a forest or marsh for they could no longer find the conditions of temperature and moisture to which they, as a group, had become adapted.

There are sunny areas in every neighborhood. They may be open spaces that serve as parks, golf courses, lawns, fields. Many plants and animals shown on the following pages are common to all these open places.

Fields are necessary to people. In them people grow food, fatten livestock, raise the plants and animals that provide our food and clothing. The pages that follow will show you how much people depend on fields.

11

Above It Are Air and Sunlight

Without air and sunlight, life in a field would suffocate and die. Air consists of gases that fill every bit of space above and around us. There are even many below us. These gases are always in motion. They hold substances which all living things need to survive.

Air is made up of nitrogen (78 per cent), oxygen (20 per cent), and other gases (2 per cent), including carbon dioxide, one of the most essential gases. It also has in it varying amounts of water vapor.

Oxygen is a gas that plants and animals use directly in breathing, or respiration. The oxygen combines with other substances to produce power or energy. So long as there are green plants and sunlight there is oxygen, because plants give off much more oxygen in photosynthesis* than they take in during respiration.

Nitrogen is plentiful, but it cannot be used by animals and ordinary plants in its pure form. It must be in combination with other substances; that is, it must be in the form of a compound. Certain soil bacteria take in nitrogen

and make compounds from it that can be absorbed by plants. From these, plants make proteins that are then eaten by both animals and man.

Carbon dioxide, a small proportion of the air, is essential to life because plants need it in making sugar and other foods. The sugar is needed for the growth of plants and animals. Carbon dioxide is kept in the air by the breathing of animals (which give out this gas as a waste), and by the decay of animal and plant matter.

Water Vapor is the gaseous form of water which enters the air by evaporation from the ocean, rivers, and streams, and from plants, animals, and soil. When air is warm, it can hold more vapor than when it is cold. If vapor-laden air suddenly cools, the water in it changes from a gas to drops of liquid which form clouds. Within the clouds the drops grow. As more vapor particles and other drops join them, they become too big to float. Then they fall as rain.

*See Page 16

Below It Is Soil

Weather has been crumbling rock for many ages. Heat expands rock, cold contracts it, cracks open up, water seeps in and later freezes, the cracks widen and fragments of rock break off. These tumble down mountains and are rolled and knocked about by the force of running water and the crash of waves upon the shore. The rock fragments are ground to fine gravel, sand, clay, and silt.

Soil contains these small rock particles plus plants and animals, both living and dead. A mere thimbleful of soil holds millions of microscopic plants and animals; a spadeful will have hundreds large enough to see without a lens — insects, their eggs and larvae, roundworms, earthworms, mites, centipedes and many others. These help keep the soil loose and add to its fertility.

The topsoil is the most fertile. It contains the most life and the most decaying matter. This is the good, growing part of the soil and one of man's most valuable possessions. Since topsoil is at the surface, it is easy to lose. Rains will wash it down hill; winds will blow it away. Loss of topsoil makes for poor land, poor crops and poor people. Topsoil varies in depth from a few inches to several feet. How deep is yours? The dark colored layer at the surface is the topsoil. The more compact soil below, with less organic matter, is lighter in color. This is the subsoil.

Water, too, is an important part of soil. Rain, falling on bare ground, runs off the surface, but is caught by plant-covered ground and soaks in. The water accumulates between the particles of soil to form an underground reservoir. The reservoir may rest on a layer of impervious rock or dense fine clay. The top of the reservoir is called the water table. To water our crops and to keep water in our streams and wells, it is essential to keep the level of the water table high.

Plants and Animals Live There

A field holds millions of plants, the food factories upon which animals depend. So close is the interdependence of animals and plants that we say, "All flesh is grass."

Plants alone have the ability to trap energy from the sun, and even they can catch less than 2 per cent of it. The green substance in plants is chlorophyll. This material absorbs energy from the sun which is used to combine carbon dioxide with water from the soil. The product that results is sugar. Later, this sugar may be combined with minerals from the soil to become proteins, fats, or other nutrients. Plants carry on this food-making only in the presence of sunlight, and it is called *photosynthesis*.

Plants use their sugar as food, which is then changed to energy or new tissue. The energy is passed on to the animals that eat plants. Energy can be stored indefinitely. When we burn coal for fuel, we are using the energy that has been stored in plants for ages.

Most of the insects, birds, and mammals of the field feed directly on some part of the green plant. The flesh-eating animals get their nourishment indirectly by feeding on the tissue of plant-eating animals.

Animals also help plants. They plow up and aerate the soil by their movement; they dig underground tunnels that become channels for water; and they help to scatter pollen and seeds that start new plants growing. Animals give their waste and skeletal remains to the soil; thus important substances are restored to the ground.

From soil to plant to animal and back to soil — that is the cycle of life.

Spring in the Fields

Warmer weather, longer days, and plenty of water lead to increased activity in the field. Seeds and other plants that have lain dormant all winter begin to grow. Gradually the fields lose the brown and straw tones of late fall and winter and take on a covering of fresh new greens.

Spring is the time of awakening, the season when most young are born. It is a time of lengthening days and of warming winds. It is a time of abundant rainfall, of rushing streams, and of puddles and mud. Field plants are beginning to awaken. The green blades of grass and flowering plants push their way through the soil.

Animals also begin to reappear. The migrating birds are returning to nest. We can hear the songs of birds, announcing their return. Bees, wasps, and butterflies begin their "ballet" of nectar-sipping by flitting from flower to flower. Because they carry pollen grains from one flower to another, the insects help to bring about pollination.

New sounds return to the countryside in spring. We hear the sound of spring freshets, the singing of many birds, the croaking of frogs and toads. We can smell the damp grassy odor of greening fields.

17

Summer in the Fields

Plants furnish abundant supplies of seeds that are food for wildlife as well as the start of new plants. For example, in one season a single red clover yields about 500 seeds; a crabgrass plant produces about 90,000 seeds. There will not be room for all these new plants. Many will be crowded out. Large quantities of seeds will be consumed by animals. In spite of the great number of seeds produced, the number of plants grown in the field each year will never be more than the field has space to accommodate.

The decaying plants of summer provide food for hordes of bacteria and fungi, the sanitation crew of the plant world. By their action, the soil gets back some of the substances "borrow-

ed" from it by the plants.

The change from mild spring to warm summer is gradual, and during this time the living things of the fields grow to adulthood. Rabbits, mice, snakes, birds, and insects are in abundance, seeking food. Butterflies by day and moths by night search for nectar. Birds are constantly hunting for seeds, earthworms, and grasshoppers, as food for themselves and their young.

As summer moves into the month of August, there is intense heat and dry weather. Flowers come into full bloom. Plants slow down their growth and begin to use stored-up moisture in the underground water supply. The plants are forming seeds from which new generations will grow.

Autumn in the Fields

Autumn is the season of maturity. Plants slow up the growing process and store their manufactured food in seeds, stems, or roots. Farmers harvest the ripened seeds. The green color disappears from plants. As the chlorophyll breaks up, other pigments present in the leaves and stems begin to show. Some leaves become yellow, bright red, or deep magenta. Gradually the plants become brown and dry. The seeds and the roots of certain plants will winter over. Here and there, hugging the ground, are rosettes of new leaves of thistle, mullein, dandelion, and a few others. These rosettes, too, will rest until spring.

Autumn is harvest time for animals. They have gathered their food and are getting ready for the cold season ahead. They begin to disappear from view. Most insects die after having laid their eggs. In some species, females or fertilized eggs winter over. Young moths winter in cocoons. Monarch butterflies migrate southward.

In the fall, most of the field birds also gather for their long journey south. They travel over instinct-directed routes to warmer regions, where they can find food until they are ready to return the following spring.

Winter in the Fields

Here is a view of life in the field during the winter. This is a season of stillness, when most life is in suspension. In some fields, there is a covering of snow; in others, the earth's surface becomes solid as the moisture in it turns to ice.

Above the ground there may still be some seeds to scatter when the wind shakes the dry plant stalks. A few hardy birds, as the juncos in the picture, find enough food to keep alive over the winter. Rabbits, quail, and a few other animals can survive the scarcities of the season if they can find food and shelter from storms and from their enemies.

Underground there is another world. The roots of plants and the fallen seeds lie dormant. Insect eggs, immature insects, and a few adults are completely inactive. As you go farther down, you find some of the "cold-blooded" animals hibernating where soil temperatures remain above freezing. Toads, snakes, and earthworms have burrowed deepest and have gone into a winter-conditioning stage. Their body activities slow down to a minimum until spring. Some warm-blooded animals hibernate, too. The mole is active day and night all through the year. In very cold weather he tunnels deeper, where the digging is easier in soil that is not frozen.

Even though winter is a time of bleakness and scarcity, it is an interesting and important season. Those creatures that survive its rigors will repopulate the fields next spring.

We can use the winter months to advantage. We can study animal shelters and cocoons; we can learn to recognize trees and shrubs by their outlines, bark, and twigs; we can track footprints in the snow to distinguish the hardy animals that stay active all winter; and we can add to their food supply and help to assure their survival.

CHAPTER II

Plants That Live in the Field

Plant life sustains all other life. Green plants alone have the power to make food from substances found in the air and soil. The food is used by both plants and animals. They do this in the presence of sunlight, by a process called photosynthesis. Plants can also make proteins and fats.

The green blades of grass and the green leaves of the trees hold the energy trapped from sunlight. Animals use this energy when they feed on plants. Microscopic bacteria break down plant matter by decay and restore the elements to the soil.

On the following pages are some examples of field plants. It is not possible to show here the species of flowers, grasses, and shrubs that grow in every region of the United States. But wherever they grow, plants sustain animals; and where both plants and animals live, man can live.

An Introduction to Plants

There are thousands of different species of plants, ranging from the microscopic one-celled bacteria and algae, to tall trees. Botanists have long grouped plants as follows: first, the *thallophytes,* which include bacteria, algae, and fungi; secondly, the *bryophytes,* made up of mosses and liverworts; thirdly, the *pteridophytes,* which include ferns, horsetails, clubmosses, and other plants; and, finally the *spermatophytes,* or seed-bearing plants.

Here is a cross-section of a typical seed-bearing plant, the most abundant of all plant groups:

1. The roots grow downward below the ground. They anchor the plant and send out many branching hairs. The roots hairs absorb the substances in water and air and pass them upward to the leaves.

2. The stem is the stalk that contains many tubes. It is the backbone of the plant, firm enough to hold up branching stems, leaves, and flowers. Raw materials from the roots travel upward through the tubes in the stem; manufactured sugar moves downward through other tubes.

3. The leaves are an expanded part of the stem, where the food-making goes on. Inside each leaf cell is chlorophyll, which is essential to the manufacture of food. After the food is produced, it is sent through the stem to be changed to new tissue or energy, or for storage.

4. The flower, which is the organ of reproduction, makes the seeds. The flower is the most attractive, most colorful and most fragrant part of most plants. See page 12 for more about flowers and seeds.

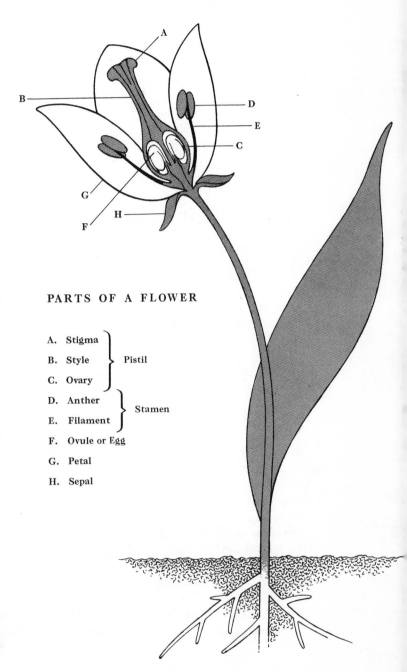

PARTS OF A FLOWER

A. Stigma ⎫
B. Style   ⎬ Pistil
C. Ovary   ⎭

D. Anther   ⎫
E. Filament   ⎬ Stamen

F. Ovule or Egg

G. Petal

H. Sepal

Plants That Man Puts to Work

Among the most simple and basic kinds of plants are the one-celled bacteria. Each can perform in its single cell many of the functions of plants with billions of cells, but bacteria lack chlorophyll. Each bacterium, like all other living cells, consists of a cell wall and a jelly-like liquid called protoplasm. Each cell can take in food matter, digest it and change it to living matter. When the cell becomes too large, it splits in half and forms two new bacteria, each with its own cell wall and protoplasm.

Because of their unusual ability to decay dead matter, bacteria are important and beneficial to plant and animal life. But their chemical action can cause decay that is harmful as well. Scientists are finding many ways in which to put bacteria to work for man. Cheese, butter, buttermilk, vinegar and sour pickles are some products that are flavored by bacterial action.

The nitrogen-fixing bacteria shown here is one type that is useful to the soil. They attach themselves to the roots of certain plants, such as legumes. The red clover is one of the most useful legumes. Farmers plant it to improve their fields and feed their cattle.

Read from the bottom up and move toward the left. Imagine that you are changing the lens of your microscope to a less powerful one with each view. First you see the bacteria; then the cells in which they grow; then the nodules that appear as swellings on the roots; and finally the whole plant. As the bacteria digest their food, they change nitrogen to a form which plants are readily able to absorb.

NITROGEN-FIXING BACTERIA

CLOVER PLANT

ENLARGEMENT OF ROOT NODULES

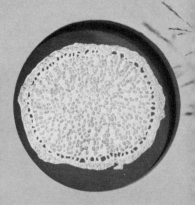

ENLARGEMENT OF NODULE

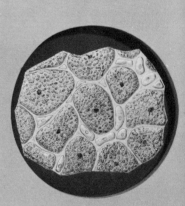

ENLARGEMENT OF CELLS
IN A NODULE

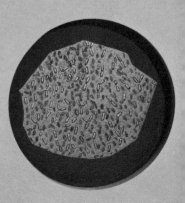

ENLARGEMENT OF BACTERIA
WITHIN THE CELL

Bacteria enter roots from the soil and establish themselves in cells of the root tissues. These cells become enlarged and finally nodules are formed. The enclosed bacteria fix nitrogen into nitrates which are released when the roots decay.

Mushrooms, Plants Without Chlorophyll

There are simple forms of plant life known as fungi. They do not contain chlorophyll, and so cannot manufacture sugar. Some fungi are parasites and get their nourishment by living on or inside the bodies of other plants or animals.

Most mushrooms are fungi that live on dead matter instead of living matter. They are called "saprophytes." In making use of dead matter as food, they work on it chemically and further decompose it. In this way they hasten the return of nutrients to the soil.

The parts of the mushroom that can be seen above the ground are only the spore-bearing parts. The mushroom has a broad mass of fine threads growing underground. This is the part that furthers decay of dead matter and is important in soil building.

The plant develops from tiny spores and may take many months to form. Then, almost before your eyes, after a heavy rain has fallen, the fleshy spore-bearing part pushes its "umbrella" above ground.

The fleshy mushroom plant is good food for squirrels, turtles, skunks, and moles. The mushrooms in this picture are edible for people, too, and contain nourishing minerals and vitamins. It is unwise to pick and taste wild mushrooms or toadstools unless you know them well because some are extremely poisonous.

Mushrooms grown for markets are usually cultivated in caves or darkened sheds. They are grown in great layers of beds on racks. Moist fertilized soil is provided and exhausted quickly by the fast-growing fungi.

Some Flowers Need Insects

Seed-bearing plants depend upon insects, birds, and winds to help them multiply their own kind. Wherever there are flowers, there are usually insects at work in search of nectar. As the insects and birds move about they carry pollen grains from one flower to another.

The flower is the reproductive part of the plant. A typical flower has a delicate *stamen* (male part), and a *pistil* (female part). The stamen is a long, slender filament topped by a pollen-bearing anther. Pollen are tiny grains of the male substance. At the top of the pistil is the stigma and at the base an ovary. Inside the ovary are "eggs" or a female substance. The pollen grain must unite with the egg before the egg can develop into a seed (see illustration page 23).

Pollen from the stamen must be transferred, somehow, to the stigma. In some species the stamens and pistils are in separate flowers. Even where both stamens and pistils are in the same flower, the pollen from another flower must be carried to the stigma. Each kind of flower has its own scheme or adaptation for getting itself pollinated.

Pollination is the transfer of the pollen grain to the stigma. There it must germinate and produce a pollen tube, which eventually reaches the female substance, or egg, in the ovary. Through this tube swims the sperm or male substance. When the sperm and egg unite, the egg is fertilized. The ovary wall begins to thicken, and a seed is formed. Each seed contains the nourishment to start a new plant of its own kind if given the proper temperature, light, and moisture.

The western anemone is one of the flowers with wide heads that attract short-tongued insects to pollinate them. Other flowers like the red clover, need the help of long-tongued bumblebees.*

*See Page 54

Wildflowers
of the Field: Daisies

In any field left undisturbed, flowers such as daisies, goldenrod, and asters are likely to be found. These plants are called perennial plants. Each year the parts above the ground die out, but their roots, bulbs, or underground stems remain alive. New plants grow from these parts the next year and will keep on growing indefinitely.

Daisies are among the most beloved of wildflowers. Some species were introduced by the colonists when they settled in the United States. As daisies tend to close their heads at night they were originally called "day's eye," from which their present name has come.

Daisies, black-eyed susans, and sunflowers are really composite flowers, each made up of many individual flowers. In the center of the daisy is a clus-

ter of individual disc flowers, each with a pistil and a stamen producing pollen. The "petals" are a group of individual ray flowers, each containing a female part or pistil. The plants depend on insects to carry pollen from one flower to another for pollination. Hundreds of tiny flowers bunched together in a kind of bouquet produce a large flowering head which attracts insects.

Daisies and other composite flowers grow in abundance. This is because they are hardy plants and can produce millions of new seeds in a single field. If you pick some for your home it will not be a great loss to the field. But the wildflowers that should not be picked take several years to mature and produce only a few seeds in one season. In each community there are wildflowers that are protected, such as the Turk's cap lily, trillium, and others.

Pods Bursting in Air

The milkweed is an attractive plant of the field, sometimes called a weed. Someone has said a weed is a plant that grows in a place where we would rather have some other plant. But many plants that grow in uncultivated fields serve a good purpose. They hold down the topsoil, thus helping to build up a better soil. They also serve as food and shelter for wildlife.

Milkweed is a tall plant that may reach a height of about five feet. Its thick, large leaves grow in pairs, each

facing opposite directions. As a result, each leaf is exposed to sunlight. The flowers are pink, lavender, or, in some species, orange. Deep inside is the sweet nectar, food for long-tongued insects. This plant is named for its milky liquid, a kind of latex that oozes out when the stem is broken. It seems to be a substance used by the plant to cover surface wounds.

In the fall the fertilized flowers produce tough seed pods, shown here in the small insert picture. The seeds appear as if they were laid evenly like shingles on a roof. When the pods are ripe, they split open at the "seam" and send forth their seeds. After the silky threads dry out, the seeds float off like tiny parachutes to find a place to grow. The silk of the mildweed is very fine, and was used during World War II as a lining in aviators' jackets and as a filler in life jackets.

Milkweed is the feeding plant of monarch butterflies in the caterpillar stage. In fact, those insects are sometimes called milkweed butterflies.

"Leaflets Three, Let It Be"

Some of the plants that serve wildlife are unpopular with people. Among these are the poison ivy (common in eastern United States), poison oak (found chiefly in the far west), and poison sumac (found in wooded swamps). The first two are plants that climb tree trunks or spread over rocks and along roadsides. They all contain a fluid that is irritating to the skin of human beings but not to wildlife.

Poison ivy (shown here) and poison sumac berries, in fact, are excellent food for wildlife in winter, because their berries stay on the plant and can be reached above the layer of snow.

Poison ivy has bright, shiny green leaves, each made up of three leaflets. The berries are usually white or gray. *Poison oak* resembles poison ivy, but it has more round-lobed leaves. It may grow taller in the shrub stage and may then attach itself to a tree-trunk and climb to the top. *Poison sumac* grows like a small tree but is restricted to wet places and has seven to eleven leaflets. Harmless forms of sumac grow in dry fields and along roadsides. They can be distinguished by long, narrow-toothed leaflets and by red clusters of berries. Poison sumac leaflets are rounded and have smooth edges like those of white ash. It is not likely to be found in fields.

The best way to avoid the skin rash from these plants is to recognize them and avoid them. A thorough washing with yellow laundry soap may prevent the rash if you know you have been exposed. When the rash appears, a paste of baking soda and water may give relief. Your doctor can recomment further treatment if necessary.

Cultivated and Uncultivated Grasses

When the first European settlers moved westward in the New World, they traveled for hundreds of miles across prairie land, where wild grasses grew thick and tall. The colonists were able to start a new life, with good grazing land for their cattle and rich topsoil for their food crops.

Fields that are left as grasslands become fertile because the decay from the plants and their way of growing in thick bunches produce a fine sod. There are some kinds of grasses that can grow in poor soil because they need little moisture and can withstand the heat and glare of strong sunlight. Such grasses grow on the slopes of the western mountains. Large herds of beef cattle graze there and are sometimes moved from one feeding range to another.

Grasses are the most nourishing of flowering plants. Their seeds, stems, and roots serve as food for many of the insects, birds, and small mammals. Some strains of grasses have been developed that produce tall and abundant crops. Some of these cultivated plants are resistant to disease and destructive insects. The crop of Suiter Fescue grass shown here is a cultivated grass. It is on such crops that many herds of dairy and beef cattle are fed.

Legumes, which are not grasses, are usually grown among grasses. They include clover, alfalfa, and sainfoin. They are good feed for cattle and help enrich soil.

Cereal Plants

Grasses also serve as important food for people. Wheat, corn, oats, rye, and barley are cereal grasses that are harvested to produce flour and many other cereal products. These cultivated grasses are grown in huge quantities with the aid of complicated machines.

Most of the farmlands of today were once thick forests or thick-sodded prairies. As our population increased, there developed a greater demand for wheat, especially during the world wars. Wheat became the chief grass crop because of the ready markets and good profits.

To grow this and other cereal crops, farmers had to plow up the topsoil. This loosened the rich sod and exposed the fertile soil to erosion by wind and rain. In some areas vast acres were stripped bare of topsoil. The bare spaces between row crops, such as corn, also helped to speed erosion.

Farmers have now learned how to grow good crops without sacrificing the topsoil. Here is a fine example of soil conservation on a farm where crops were planned ahead. The farmer planted forage crops for animal food, between the strips of corn and wheat. Strip plantings and contour plowing assure a good soil for many years to come. The rotation of cereal and legume crops, such as clover, keeps the fields supplied with nitrogen.

The trees that dot the landscape also hold down the topsoil. They provide shelter and food for birds and mammals which, in turn, play their part in controlling the number of insects and weeds. It is the hedges along the margins of fields, however, that provide the best cover and food for wildlife.

Shrubs of the Fields

Good grass land prepares the soil for larger plants. Shrubs are such plants. They grow taller than grasses and flowers and have woody stems that grow longer each year. They are known as woody plants.

Blackberry, barberry, blueberry, sumac, and wild roses are some common shrubs of the field. They are sometimes found at the edge of a woods, where field and forest meet. Shrubs prepare the ground for forest trees.

The multiflora rose hedge in the picture was planted by the farmer as a border for a contoured corn crop. This fencerow serves as a windbreak to hold down the soil. It also keeps out grazing cattle. It is fast-growing, needs little care, and has some value for attracting wildlife. Shrubs make good cover and food for meadowlarks, pheasants, bobolinks, and quail. In season, these birds are joined by catbirds, song sparrows, goldfinches and other song birds that consume their share of insects and weed seeds. Their bright colors and songs also bring pleasure to the people nearby.

Mammals, such as the white-footed mice, short-tailed shrews, and cottontail rabbits, live among the fencerows. The plants also provide cover for larger mammals, the skunks, foxes and raccoons that prey on the mice and rabbits, which would otherwise become too numerous and eat too many crops.

In the Shade of the Old Apple Tree

The largest plants of the field are the trees. They are found on field borders where they have not been plowed up. On the Great Plains, or North American prairie, trees are not generally found because of insufficient rainfall. In more humid areas, trees grow in fields abandoned by man.

This apple tree may have been planted, or it may have been grown from a seed that was dropped by some bird or by some animal feeding on an apple. The twisted branches of this tree and its decayed hollows are the favorite nesting places of woodpeckers and bluebirds. A single tree like this one provides shade and cover for grazing cows or even for the farmer himself on a summer day. It holds down a large quantity of soil and conserves moisture deep under the earth. Its fallen leaves enrich the soil when they decay.

Most trees grow best where there is plenty of sunlight and moisture. They grow slowly in the shade of other trees. Common trees of the field are the elm, the hawthorn, and the wild cherry.

Perhaps thick forest land once covered these hillsides. As people needed space for farming, they cut away trees to raise crops. Instead of clearing away all the trees, many farmers now leave a woodlot as a windbreak and as a shelter for wildlife. On the other hand, an untended field after many years may develop into a thick forest.

CHAPTER III

Cold-blooded Animals of the Field

AN INTRODUCTION TO ANIMALS

The animals shown on the following pages are called cold-blooded animals, but this is really a misnomer. They represent the forms of animal life that have no mechanism for regulating the body temperature. The temperature inside the bodies of these animals is the same as that outside. When it is cold outside, the blood inside these animals is cold; when it is hot outside, their blood is hot.

Included in this chapter is one representative of the Annelida, an earthworm; and one of the Arachnida, a spider. All of the other invertebrate animals shown are insects. They have no spinal cord. A few cold-blooded vertebrates included here are the toad, turtle, and snake.

Animals do their share in keeping fields fertile. Some live underground and help to aerate the soil; some fly among the flowers, spreading pollen dust which helps new seeds grow; some bury seeds for food and help to establish new plants. The wastes and skeletons of animals decompose and restore needed substances to the soil.

Plants and animals have a common principle of structure. Each is made of living cells, and each keeps alive by an interchange with its environment. All living things breathe, take in food substances, digest food, build tissue, and reproduce their own kind. Plants cannot move about in search of food and cover, but they can perform the most basic function of all. They alone can take the simple gases and minerals and transform them into a manufactured food. Animals eat this food directly or indirectly.

Animals can move about. They crawl, swim, walk, hop, or fly to get food. They are also equipped with a nervous system that controls their sense of sight, sound, touch, smell, and taste. Animals have a kind of intelligence, which warns them of danger and helps them to perform complicated acts. For example, they build strong nests for their young; they remain motionless at a time of danger; or they even feign being wounded if an intruder is near.

AN INTRODUCTION TO INSECTS

More insects have been classified by man than any other group of animals. They are the chief source of food of many other animals. They can be recognized by the following body structures:

a) Six legs
b) A three-part body
c) Usually one or two pairs of wings
d) Feelers, or antennae
e) An external skeleton

On the *head* of insects are the mouth parts, the eyes and the feelers or antennae. The legs are attached to the midsection or *thorax*. The *abdomen* holds the organs of digestion, the spiracles for breathing, and the organs of excretion and reproduction. Some female insects have long, slender ovipositors at the end of the abdomen, with which they dig a hole in the ground to deposit their eggs.

Insects develop by a complete or an incomplete metamorphosis, which means change of form. When the young insects (nymphs) hatch out of the eggs looking like tiny replicas of their parents, their development is called incomplete. Many species of insects go through four distinct stages before they mature, and in each stage they change their appearance. First they are eggs, then larvae, then pupae, and finally, adults. This is a complete metamorphosis.

Insects are very abundant. They can live and feed in water, under water, over water; in the air; on the ground, under the ground; and in the trees. They multiply in large numbers. Yet, when cold weather approaches most insects die. Only the eggs, the larvae or the fertilized females may remain alive to carry on the species.

So vast is the science of insect study, or entomology, that it is subdivided into medical entomology (the study of disease and insects), economic entomology (the control of destructive insects on farms and in industry), and other categories.

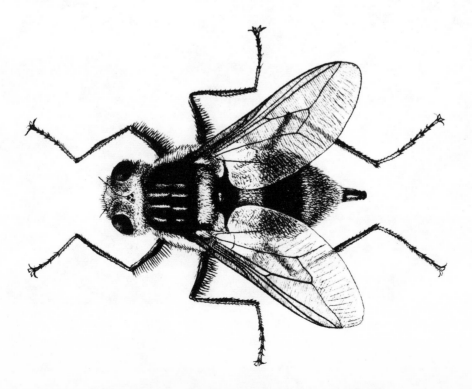

The Grasshopper

The grasshopper is a typical insect because, when we examine it, we can readily distinguish its three-part body; the three pairs of legs, the antennae, and the large eyes.

The bulging eyes of the grasshopper are the compound eyes. Each eye is made up of many lenses, fitted together like the cells of a honeycomb. In some insects, usually those with short feelers, the compound eyes may have thousands of lenses. These eyes help the insect to see in all directions. Between the compound eyes are three small eyes that are useful only for sensing light and dark. The hearing part of the grasshopper is located in the abdomen.

Grasshoppers are well adapted to live among the grasses. Their jaws are shaped for biting off leaves and grinding them. Their hind legs have long thighs, within which are strong muscles that help them jump high. Tiny claws at the end of each leg help the insects to cling to the smooth blades of grass.

Grasshoppers do not build nests, nor does the female need to care for the young. She deposits the fertilized eggs in the ground late in the fall in a hole dug out with her ovipositor. The eggs remain there over the winter, and in the spring tiny grasshopper nymphs emerge. They are able to hop about in search of food soon after hatching.

Grasshopper populations are normally kept in check by the field animals that feed on them: tiny red mites, hawks, skunks, toads, and snakes.

The Praying Mantis Hunts His Prey

One relative of the grasshopper family is a flesh-eater and feeds on a variety of other insects. He is the praying mantis. When he is at rest, the mantis keeps his long forelegs folded, and he resembles a *praying* individual. A more accurate name for him might be the *preying* mantis.

The mantis can turn his head better than most insects. The small, triangular-shaped head and the bulging eyes help him to see all around him. His front legs are long and sharply bent, better adapted for catching an insect than for walking. Inside the first two sections of these legs are sharp spines that help to hold down the food.

The praying mantis is a good example of camouflage in nature. His body, legs, and wings take on the color of the leaves. In the summer the insect is a vivid green; in fall its color changes to olive brown. Even the egg cases, left on the tall grasses over the winter, take on the color of the plants.

The mantis consumes large numbers of smaller insects, either in the nymph or in the adult stages. It is said that the female devours the male mantis after mating in late summer. If this is true, it may have begun way back in history when insects could find little food. It was more important for the female who carried the eggs to survive, and the male may have had to be eliminated to conserve food.

If you collect a mantis egg case in winter, keep it in a box outdoors until spring. You will be able to see the tiny nymphs emerge and crawl off in search of insect food.

Insects We Can Hear: The Katydid and the Grasshopper

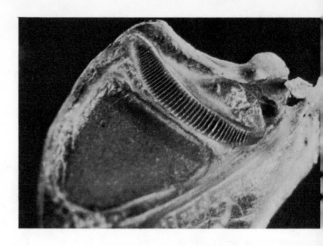

The katydid and the grasshopper are related members of the Orthoptera group of insects. The male has a way of producing sounds, and the reason he does this is still uncertain. Maybe he is in good spirits, or is trying to out-sing a neighbor. Maybe he makes noise just to attract a female.

The male grasshopper rubs his long hind legs like a bow over the outer wings. This makes a rasping kind of music. He may alternate legs and wings or even do both together in a kind of "duet."

The katydid, shown below is a green insect, living high in the trees. His bright green wing covers resemble the leaves and the flying wings are folded beneath them, like fans. The katydid has longer feelers than the grasshopper, and his eyes are not so bulging. His hearing parts are located in the front leg, while those of the grasshopper are under his wings on the abdomen. Katydids are, therefore, said to "hear with their elbows."

Male katydids produce sounds at night, especially during warm weather. The sound is produced through a banjo-like arrangement at the base of the wings. The insert picture above shows the file or ridged surface that is found at the base of the left front wing. The right wing holds a small scraper, used as a pick. The insect rubs his left wing over the right quickly to make a distinctive sound. A bulge on either side of the sound-making parts serves as an amplifier. The structure directs the sound, so that when the insect is facing us, the noise is much louder than when he is turned away. Katydids usually chirp in a vertical position, with heads down.

The Ground Cricket

Although the ground cricket is an Orthoptera, it does not fly like the katydid, nor does it climb like the grasshopper. It hops on the ground among the grasses; its wings are rather short stumps, but its hind legs are strong. Crickets are easily recognized because of their black, slippery skin. If you catch a male, keep him in a ventilated jar with grass and leaves and he will chirp for you.

The cricket in the picture is a female, distinguished by the long, thin organ at the back, which is the ovipositor.

The male cricket has musical parts on his wing covers. He has a file and a scraper, but they are both on each wing. He can rub either wing over the other and produce sound. The right file, rubbing against the scraper of the left wing, causes the chirping sound, as does the left file, rubbing against the scraper of the right wing. It is possible that some of the sounds made by crickets are lost to us, because they may be in the ultra-high frequency range which cannot be heard by human ears.

In mid-summer, tree crickets keep up a constant chirp. They sing at night, and their sounds are repeated more often when the temperature is higher. If you are kept awake by a tree cricket, here is a practical way of falling asleep. Count the number of chirps in 15 seconds, and add 40. You will have learned the approximate temperature of the place where the cricket is at the moment and the counting will put you to sleep.

The Common Cicada

Much of the noise in August comes from the trilling of the cicadas. Male cicadas have a large pair of plates on the underside at the base of the abdomen. Strong muscles on these plates vibrate and release the plates with a snap. A cavity inside the abdomen acts as a sounding board, making the noise appear louder. Cicadas trill during the hottest hours of the summer day.

The dog-day or harvest fly cicada, shown here, bears young each year. The eggs are deposited on the stems of plants. When they hatch, the larvae fall to the ground and feed on plant roots and water until they mature. The young cicada in the picture has moved out of its outgrown skin. After about four years, the insect is fully grown and spends its days trilling from the tree tops.

One species of cicada needs from thirteen to seventeen years to develop. It is known as the periodical cicada. Its larvae stay underground during all these years, feeding on root juices. When the young are ready to emerge, they dig their way toward the surface and usually climb some object (as a tree). After their wings dry out, they can fly. They may live only a few days above ground, just long enough to mate and deposit their eggs in the ground.

During the cicada season, many birds and insects gather to feast on them. One kind of wasp, the cicada-killer wasp, stings its prey into a state of paralysis and drags it to its burrow as food for its young.

Aphids, Insect "Cows"

The tiny green insects commonly called plant lice are aphids. They breed by the millions each season and feed on the sap of roots, stems, twigs, and leaves. They suck the sap and convert it into a food and waste substance called honeydew. Ants and other insects are fond of this honeydew. Ants tend aphids and "milk" them by gently stroking them. The honeydew is used for food for the ants' grubs.

Each spring, millions of aphid eggs hatch out and the young nymphs begin to feed on plant sap. The tiny creatures are all females, capable of laying eggs without mating.

When the food seems to be giving out, a brood of aphids with wings de-velops. They fly out and start a new colony on another plant. Toward fall, winged male and female aphids hatch. In the adult stage, the aphids fly out and mate in the air. The males die at once. The females die after they have deposited their eggs. These shiny black oval eggs are all that remain in winter to carry on the aphid species.

Fortunately for the plants of farm or garden, large numbers of aphid eggs do not hatch. Many of the young are destroyed by tiny parasites, animals that feed on the bodies of other animals; other aphid nymphs are eaten by the young of ladybird beetles and lacewing flies. Flycatchers, chickadees, and other birds also feed on aphids.

Beetles

Beetles are among the most numerous insects. They occur nearly everywhere in many shapes and sizes. They are distinguished by a hard pair of outer wings that act as covers protecting the soft flying wings beneath. Most beetles have rounded, thick bodies that are shiny and smooth.

Farmers know insects by their feeding habits, and this knowledge helps them to control insects. One species of ladybird beetle, shown here, was brought over from Australia to help overcome an invasion of destructive insects in the citrus groves of the West Coast. Each ladybird beetle consumes many times its weight in insect food, and these beetles saved the crops. They have been saving crops ever since. Ladybird beetles are found throughout the United States and parts of Canada.

Some species of beetles, however, are not so welcome. The Colorado potato beetle (inset) enjoys the bounty of cultivated potato farms and has multiplied until it is now a "pest." Before the coming of the white man to our country, this insect lived in the western mountains and fed on a wild plant related to the potato plant. When people began to farm potatoes, the beetles moved in. As the cultivation of this crop increased, the numbers of potato beetles increased. They roamed unchecked across the land, far from their original habitat. Insecticides are now necessary to keep their number controlled.

The Monarch Butterfly: Egg and Larva

One of the most beautiful insects to adorn the summer landscape is the monarch butterfly. It is common in fields throughout northern United States and Canada. The pictures on the next few pages give close-up photographs of the four stages through which a butterfly passes before it matures. This process takes about a month, and in each stage the butterfly takes on a different form as is common in insects with a complete metamorphosis. Moths pass through similar stages.

In late spring the female monarch lays her first brood of eggs on the underside of milkweed leaves. Each egg looks like a little green pearl. Soon a tiny larva, or caterpillar, pushes its way out. It feeds on the leaves constantly. At first it is about one-eighth inch long, and as it feeds, it grows; as it grows, its skin becomes too small, and it molts. It molts four times, each time acquiring new colors. The caterpillar in the picture is in its last molt. It is green with yellow and black stripes.

The caterpillar is a worm-like creature, long and slender with a body of twelve or thirteen segments and with several pairs of legs. At the front end are three pairs of legs and at the rear

are about five pairs of "prolegs." The monarch larva is quite smooth. Its sensory extensions wave from both ends of the body, probably feeling for obstacles or other insects.

The jaws of caterpillars are well developed for the around-the-clock routine of biting and chewing leaves. They even chew up their own molted skin.

From Caterpillar to Chrysalis

About three weeks after the larva comes out of the egg, it stops eating and begins to settle down for its pupal stage, which is called the chrysalis.

The body of the insect becomes short and thick inside the shell, which hangs from the tail. It is attached by a stem of silk to a twig from which it hangs suspended for nine to twelve days.

Inside, the creature does not stir. It is undergoing many changes. The body is using up the nourishment that has been stored in the form of fat. Its digestive system is changing from one that feeds on solids to one that sips only liquids. Wings are developing. Muscles for flying are being strengthened to replace those used for crawling.

The nervous system is changing, and sex organs are forming.

Through the transparent shell we can already see the change that has taken place. The black and yellow spots are visible, and the wing structure is complete.

It is possible that the bitter flavor of the milkweed plant makes the monarch pupae and butterflies distasteful to birds. Most birds are reported to shun them as food.

The viceroy butterfly, found in the eastern and central parts of the country, resembles the monarch butterfly in coloring. This mimicry protects it from birds who might otherwise find it more delectable than the monarch.

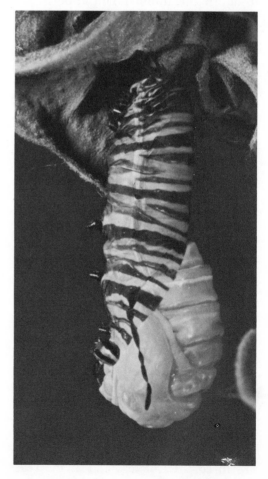

Hail to the Monarch!

It is now the dramatic moment when the butterfly is ready to emerge. The legs, "tongue," and antennae are still attached to the pupa skin. Look closely at the picture and you can see this more clearly. The pale green shell still hangs suspended from its strong silken stem.

At first the insect is limp, soft, and damp. It must wait until its skeletal structures harden and it can expand its wings before it is ready to fly away.

Monarch butterflies have a wing span of about four inches. They are reddish-brown, with black veins, black borders, and two rows of white or yellow spots at the outer edges. They are as beautiful in the adult stage as they were in the caterpillar and chrysalis stages.

Monarchs seem to have no fear of hungry animals as they fly boldly among the flowers. They feed by sucking in nectar through their hollow tongue, or proboscis. This is coiled when not in use and uncoils to probe deeply inside a flower. As it searches for nectar, the insect helps to pollinate the flowers.

Such is the development of the monarch butterfly. Many of the eggs never develop into butterflies. The eggs, larvae, or pupae are eaten by birds, beetles, and other animals. The young may also be destroyed by tiny parasites that thrive inside their bodies.

The Monarch Butterfly, Winter Migrant

Here is a mass of monarch butterflies that have gathered in the fall of the year for migration to warmer regions. Most species of butterflies die after leaving eggs, larvae, or pupae in sheltered places for the winter. But not the monarch. It has an unusual habit of migrating, which is still not fully understood.

These butterflies travel the same route each year, each generation knowing by instinct where to fly and where to rest. Trees along the route, known as "butterfly trees," like the one in the picture, attract the monarchs each year. Scientists believe that butterflies recognize these trees by their scent. Through a scent pocket the male monarch gives off a faint odor which attracts females. When thousands of butterflies assemble on a tree at night to rest they remain close together and the odor is strong. There may be so many insects on a single tree that it is weighted down. The odor from those butterflies is probably strong enough to remain on the trees, guiding each year's migrants.

The monarch butterflies return north in the spring. Their instinct leads them over the same route and their long journey ends when they find milkweed plants. This is the favorite breeding plant of the monarch butterfly. When the eggs hatch into larvae, and the larvae develop into chrysalides, and the chrysalides become mature butterflies, the new generation flies further north. These are the butterflies we see in July in most parts of the United States and Canada. They, in turn, lay eggs and hatch another brood before the fall migration.

The Black Swallowtail Butterfly

"Scaly-winged" is the name given by the early Greeks to the brilliant-hued butterflies and moths. This greatly magnified view of the wing of a black swallowtail (at right) shows the arrangement of the scales. They overlap like shingles on a roof and serve the same purpose, shielding the animal against rain. The scales are also called butterfly feathers because they tend to shed when the wing is handled.

Swallowtails mate in May and the female lays smooth, round eggs singly on the underside of leaves. The caterpillars are black and white. After four molts they become green, yellow, and black. Their orange-colored horns are scent-pockets that give off a strong odor.

The pupae rest for the winter as chrysalides attached to plant stems. The adult swallowtail can be seen among milkweed and garden flowers early in the spring. This butterfly is one of the largest species and is found throughout the United States and southern Canada. Its name is derived from its two-tail extensions. Its color is black with bright yellow spots across the wings and some blue on the hind wings.

Some species of butterfly take on a different appearance in different sections of the country. The female tiger swallowtail, for example, is dark brown in the southern states of the United States; those found up North are bright yellow. The larvae of these butterflies are noted for the black and yellow spots at the front of the body that give them the appearance of a snake.

The Sphinx Moth

Moths are the night-feeding relatives of butterflies. Like owls, skunks, earthworms, and fireflies, most moths find safety under the cover of darkness. However, there are day-flying moths, too.

A moth can be distinguished from a butterfly by its thick body. Butterflies fold their wings and hold them vertically over their backs while at rest; most moths keep their wings open horizontally. The thread-like antennae of butterflies are usually knobbed at the top. Moth antennae vary, but usually they taper to a point or are webbed like tiny feathers.

The sphinx moth is one of the large species of moths, growing to about four inches. It is ash-gray and on its thick body are five pairs of yellow spots. The young larvae feed on tomato, potato, and tobacco plants. Their number is usually not so great that they are destructive to the crops.

The sphinx moth feeds at night on the deep-tubed flowers that tend to open at dusk. One type of sphinx moth is often mistaken for a hummingbird because of its large size and its way of hovering among flowers.

The largest and most colorful are the silk-spinning moths, which include the cecropia, promethea, and luna moths. They are usually found in wooded areas.

Many different kinds of birds feed on moths and the moth larvae are preyed upon by tiny parasites.

Ants

Ants are familiar insects, busily moving about on the ground, on trees, on walls, and in crevices of homes. If we take the time to watch them, we can see that each insect is at work on a specific job.

All ants live in colonies which consist of thousands of worker ants and a single fertile queen. Some of the workers are guards; some are food-getters; some gather building materials; some stay inside the colony and tend the young ants. There are dairy ants that "milk" aphid and farmer ants that plant fungus farms and gather seeds for storage.

The worker ants are infertile females without wings. Once a year, winged ants develop and fly out for their mating flight. The males die after mating, and the females return to lay eggs. If the queen starts a new colony, she lays her eggs in a sheltered spot and cares for them herself. If she returns to an established colony, the worker ants care for the young. A queen ant need mate but once, and for ten or fifteen years she can continue to produce young.

The mound in this picture is typical of those built by Allegheny mound-builder ants, found in fields and at the edge of woods in the northeastern states. A single colony has many such mounds, which measure about one to two feet high and about three feet in diameter. If the mound is peaked and spongy to the touch, it is still in use. If you should find one that is rounded at the top and quite solid, it has been abandoned.

The constant movement of ants in search of food and shelter helps to aerate the soil and improve its fertility. Ant larvae and mature ants feed on seeds, insects, and bits of vegetable matter. Ants and ant eggs are, in turn, sought as food by many animals.

Bumblebees

Most field bees are solitary insects, living in or under the ground. Bumblebees live under the ground in colonies, with an organized system of workers, queens, and drones.

The bumblebee is a stubby black and yellow bee usually seen among bright-colored flowers. A young queen, sole survivor of her colony after the winter, starts a new nest in the spring. She often chooses the abandoned nest of a field mouse. She gathers pollen and nectar from plants and mixes these with her own juices to form a ball. When the ball is the right size, she places it in the egg-cell and lays her egg. She then fashions a cover of wax (this wax is also used for honey pots) which is placed next to the egg. When the young larvae hatch out, bee bread is waiting for them. As they feed, they dig themselves little spaces into which they fit for their pupa stage. They are encased in tough cocoons for ten days.

The queen bee is busy in early spring, building up the nest and laying eggs. When workers have grown, they take over her work of feeding and building.

The queen has only to lay eggs thereafter, and she may lay about 500 in a season. In late summer a few males (drones) and new queens develop and fly out to mate. The fertilized queens then hibernate during the winter.

The bumblebee's nest in the picture is made up of cells, honey pots, and cocoons. It is not so clean and orderly as the hives of the honeybee. The bee in the inset picture has picked up a large supply of pollen.

Bumblebees are long-tongued insects and play an important part in pollinating red clover and fruit orchards.

The Honeybee

Honeybees have a higher form of social organization than that of bumblebees. They store their honey in wax cells in a neat and orderly fashion. A hive consists of one mother or queen, thousands of workers, and a few drones. There may be 50,000 bees living in one hive, in which the workers and drones live a few months; the queen bee may live for several years.

The bees that are seen on bright-colored flowers, such as the wild rose bush in this picture, are usually worker honeybees. They are slimmer and smaller than bumblebees. Some workers go out in the fields in search of nectar and pollen; others remain in the hive to serve as builders, cleaners, and nurses. A bee may fly as much as a mile in search of flowers, yet it seems to know its way back. If a bee should stop at another colony it is chased at the entrance by the guard bees.

A German scientist, Dr. Karl von Frisch, found that bees have a way of communicating with other bees when they have found a new source of nectar. He reported that they enter the hive and "dance." From the direction in which they dance and from the duration of the dance, they seem to be telling the others how to find the new flower patch.

The queen bee lays eggs at the rate of about 2,000 a day. After one mating, she can continue laying eggs for three or four years. The young larvae are first fed by the nurse bees on royal jelly made from honey. After a few days, most larvae are fed bee bread, a mixture of pollen and nectar. Those that will become queens are continued on the diet of royal jelly. A few drones hatch out at the end of the summer. They fly out to mate with a queen before the winter comes.

An Apiary

Bees can take material from flowers and from their own bodies and manufacture a food that man likes to eat. Since Biblical times man has used honey as a sweetening. The honeybees that now thrive in all parts of the United States and Canada are descendants of bees brought over from Europe.

Bees are raised in hives from which their wax and honey are gathered and sold. Each year, beekeepers distribute about 500 million pounds of honey and about 10 million pounds of wax. Beekeepers also rent hives to fruit farmers, who release the bees to pollinate their orchards.

A beekeeper sets up boxes in an area where suitable plants grow. This assures a good quality and quantity of honey. White clover yields a delicious honey, as do wild raspberry, alfalfa, and buckwheat. The boxes consist of trays with a wax foundation, imprinted with the base of cells. The hive resembles a natural hive, and speeds up honey making, as the bees do not need to take the time to build it or make the framework for the honeycomb.

Bees use a system of division of labor during the honey-making season. Some bees fly out to the fields. They return to the hive, empty their pollen baskets and fly off again. Other workers pack the pollen into the cell. Inside the hive, bees are engaged in making honey and bee bread. An air-conditioning crew flaps its wings rapidly to create air currents. In this way, the bees control the temperature and evaporate the moisture for the production of honey.

The Paper-Making Wasp

Wasps are the earliest paper makers. They build a simple structure of paper cells in the shelter of an overhang. This paper, chewed from bits of plant material, is waterproofed from time to time by new material licked on by the female. She is in the picture.

Adult wasps usually feed on nectar or sap, while their larvae are fed insects and spiders. Some wasp larvae are so tiny that they can live as parasites inside the bodies of aphids and codling moths. Others, such as polistes larvae, feed on the larvae and mature insects of the fields and the adults do their part in pollinating flowers.

Female wasps hibernate through the winter. In the spring they build a nest and rear their young. The nest is suspended from a single stem and the cells are open at one end. The hornets and the yellow-jackets, related to these wasps, build a more elaborate enclosed structure in which they rear thousands of young.

Wasps are usually feared for their sting. They will sting only if provoked and, unlike honey bees, do not endanger their own lives when they sting. The sting comes from the egg-laying organ or ovipositor of the worker wasp. Honeybees have two barbed spears attached to an egg-shaped sac of poison. First one barb is pushed into the skin of the "enemy" and then the other. The fluid from the poison sac oozes into the space, and the skin becomes irritated. If the bee cannot take back its barbs, it must fly off and leave the sac behind. Sometimes the abdomen remains too, and the bee dies.

If you should be stung, scrape the wound with a knife blade, but do not squeeze it. Apply an ammonia solution, or cold and hot applications to relieve the swelling and pain.

The Earthworm, Plowman of the Earth

To the robin, earthworms are a delectable food; to the fisherman, they are good bait. To the soil, earthworms are little farmers that keep burrowing underground, stirring up the soil to bring in air and fertilizer. They also drag plant materials into the ground.

Charles Darwin, an English scientist who lived in the nineteenth century, studied the habits of earthworms over many years. He called them the "most valuable animals," because of their habit of swallowing soil as they burrow. Some of the organic matter is used as food. The rest is left on the surface along with the excrement as worm castings. Darwin estimated that in a year, the earthworms on one acre of ground could deposit 18 tons of castings on the surface. The castings are the little black heaps of earth around the animals in the picture shown below.

Earthworms seem simple; yet they have quite an elaborate body structure. They have a nervous system, a blood system, and a digestive system. Each worm has male and female parts, and when two individual worms come together, they fertilize each other. The body is segmented and held together by soft, flexible rings. Each segment holds four pairs of bristles with which the worm crawls and holds on to the ground as it climbs. Robins must tug and tug to lift an earthworm from the ground because of these bristles.

Earthworms seem to be able to grow new body parts if one part is cut away. Scientists in a laboratory take the front end of one worm and join it with thread to the rear end of another. A new, short worm grows and lives. Sections from three different worms will grow together and form a single long worm.

The Orange Garden Spider

Spiders, scorpions, daddy-long-legs, ticks, and mites are field creatures that cannot be classified with insects. They are Arachnids. They have eight legs and a two-part body, in which the head and thorax have grown together. They have neither antennae nor wings.

Spiders depend for nourishment on the juices that they suck from the bodies of insects. They can paralyze their prey with a poison that comes from a poison fang and is far more dangerous to insects than it is to man. The bite of a black widow is probably the most irritating to man.

Spiders spin a very fine, strong silk as an aid in snaring food. Some spin webs, as does the orange garden spider shown here. They get about among the grasses with the aid of a dragline, a thread of silk that is thrust forward, just as a mountain climber uses his lifeline. The threads we find on plants and on walls are these discarded draglines.

Spiders spin beautiful webs. In the picture we see an orb web; other species spin triangular and dome-shaped webs. The garden spider first stretches a framework around the area to be covered. Then she hangs lines to form spokes. On these she spins a framework of connecting threads and then a spiral of sticky, elastic thread that helps to hold down the prey. The spider waits, either within the web or at the side. As soon as there is a tug, she walks across the web and injects poison into the insect. She then wraps it in silken thread until she is ready to feed on it.

Spiders feed on many insects. In the web of nature, however, spiders are trapped by toads, snakes, frogs, and praying mantis.

59

Toads

Toads are amphibians, belonging to the cold-blooded group of animals that have a spinal cord and live in both land and water. Unlike the frogs, however, toads spend all of their adult life on land, except at breeding time.

The toad in the picture is a Fowler's toad, with brown skin, black spots, and reddish warts that blend well with the surrounding grasses. Toads hibernate in winter. The males emerge first in the spring. They make their way to a pond and can be heard, especially on rainy days, trilling a mating call. During mating, the female lays her eggs in water. The eggs are in long jelly strings that float. There are from 4,000 to 12,000 eggs from one toad. The tiny tadpoles that hatch out, breathe under water through gills. Later, the toads develop lungs and become land-living creatures.

Toads are distinguished from frogs by their rough skins covered with warts. Contrary to popular superstition, toads do not give warts to people who touch them. The warts are glands, used by the toad as a defense weapon. A bitter, milky liquid, secreted by these glands, probably helps keep other animals from eating toads. Hawks, crows, skunks, and snakes, however, do manage to eat them occasionally.

Because of their diet, toads are among the most useful animals in a field. They feed on large quantities of insects, such as those that feed on grass and other field crops. These are easily caught with the toad's two-inch sticky tongue, which is fastened at the front of the mouth and can be flipped outside to snap up any prey that comes too near.

The Box Turtle

The box turtle is a slow-moving reptile. The word "reptile" in Latin means crawling animal. This turtle consumes large numbers of worms, slugs, snails, insects, and some plant material.

The turtle's hard shell is its armored tank, within which it hides when alarmed. The shell, or carapace, is its backbone and skin grown together.

The box turtle has an additional protection in its undershell, or plastron. Hinges cause both the carapace and plastron to meet, enclosing the animal completely. The box turtle may be dark-brown or black with yellow spots and streaks. It may have either red, yellow, or brown eyes.

Baby turtles are less than two inches long and reach their five inch length only after five years. Box turtles live over forty years and they spend much of their time resting. In winter they hibernate to avoid the cold climate. In summer they crawl into the mud to sleep through the hottest days.

Box turtles make hardy pets. Besides insect food they eat fruit, especially bits of apple and melon. Give them raw chopped meat, water, plant food, and plenty of space in which to roam. These four pictures show how the turtle is concealed inside the carapace and how he can turn over if he should find himself turned upside-down.

Snakes of the Field

This pilot black snake is one of the hundreds of species that are not poisonous. He has no fangs, though he may scare you when he sticks out his forked tongue. This species ranges through the eastern parts of the United States, Texas, and the Great Plains. It has a smooth, satiny black skin with keeled scales. Its throat and chin are white. It is about one and a half inches in diameter and about six feet long.

Some of our most valuable snakes consume quantities of small mice. An entire litter may be taken from the nest and eaten. Small toads, frogs, and earthworms are also on the menu. Eggs and nestling birds are an occasional food for snakes. Most snakes eat many insects. Snakes are shy and usually keep out of one's way. Should you meet a harmless snake, however, it is best to leave it to carry on its food-getting which, incidentally, helps to check the number of the animals on which it preys.

Some snakes try to scare off an attacker by picking up their heads, coiling the body or flattening it and making a hissing sound. The teeth of snakes curve backward in the mouth and provide a good grip on their food. Their lower jaw is split in half, and the animal swallows the prey by alternating left and right movements of half the jaw.

The poisonous snakes, such as copperheads or rattlesnakes, have curved fangs, hollow teeth attached to a pair of poison glands. These snakes, too, are shy and crawl away when they sense danger. They bite man only in self-defense or if they are molested.

A New Generation of Snakes

Many snakes, like lizards, frogs, birds, and other animals lay eggs. From these are hatched young snakes. Some species, however, bear live young in a semi-transparent membrane through which each young snake will eventually emerge.

The brood of black snakes in the picture shows the large number of young that one female usually produces. Snake parents do not stay with their young. Almost at once, the young are able to crawl away in search of food. Young black snakes are pale gray with brownish blotches, which will disappear in the second year when the skin becomes a shiny black.

Snakes molt a few times in a season, depending on how much they eat and how often they outgrow their skins.

If you should find a snakeskin, pick it up and examine it. This is not a skeleton, but a skin that a snake shed as it grew. See the large scales on the underside that help the animal crawl. Find the skin goggles that shielded its eyes. You will notice that the skin is wrong side out. The old skin loosens first around the mouth. The snake rubs itself against sticks and stones, and gradually it wriggles out of the skin, turning it inside out as we would pull off a stocking.

Young snakes are exposed to predation by flesh-eaters, such as skunks, opossums, hawks, eagles, owls, and other snakes. The road runner, a western bird, has earned a reputation for its ability to attack, capture, and feed upon large snakes.

CHAPTER IV

Birds: Warm-blooded Animals with Feathers

Birds of the field and meadow play an important role in the balance of nature. They are busy animals and need large quantities of food to keep them supplied with energy. Some birds feed on plants; others eat insects, earthworms, snakes, mice, and other small mammals. Some feed on both plant and animal matter.

Birds are useful to fields. They spread new plants by carrying seeds from one place to another. They feed on weed seeds and wild grasses, preventing them from spreading too rapidly and too far. Their droppings add minerals and food elements to the soil. When birds die, decomposition products from their flesh and bones add other nutrients.

The insect-eating birds are useful to farmers. Imagine how many millions of eggs are laid each year by beetles, grasshoppers, moths, and other insects. What would be man's fate if all the eggs hatched and grew into new insects? Birds help to keep the insect world in control.

The bird population is also kept in check. Many of the young birds born each year do not survive; if they did, there would be too much competition for food. Young birds are subject to many dangers. They may be eaten by larger birds, snakes, or mammals; they may be destroyed by parasites feeding on them; they may be poisoned by insecticide sprays; or they may die of one of the bird diseases. The birds that do survive find enough food and shelter to keep alive for several years, and have new broods each year.

Birds are probably our most beautiful and best-loved animals. We enjoy their beautiful colors, their graceful flight, their lovely songs, and their habits of nesting and raising a family. Birds are useful, and man can profit by attracting more of them to his land.

Birds Are Streamlined for Flight

Birds fly higher and farther than any other creatures. Everything about a bird's body helps to make it a good flier: its shape, its bone structure, and its systems of breathing and circulation of blood.

The bone structure of a bird is very light in weight for the size of the animal. Some bones are filled with air spaces through which the air may circulate. The bird has an unusual combination of flexible and fused bones. For example, the bones in the backbone and breastbone are fused; the ribs and the neckbones are flexible.

The hand and wrist bones have been fused to produce a strong, rigid organ useful in flight. The breastbone, to which strong wing muscles are attached, acts as a center ridge or keel.

Birds need a great deal of energy to carry on their active lives. They get this from a high rate of food intake and rapid digestion. Rapid breathing supplies the needed oxygen for this process.

The temperature inside the body of a bird is high and is kept steady regardless of the temperature outside. A very efficient system of air-conditioning makes this possible. There are several pairs of air sacs and air tubes spread throughout the body, through which the air passes when the bird breathes.

With its strong, large heart and a good system of blood circulation, the bird can quickly change food to energy and tissue. Birds need a great deal of food as well as oxygen, with which to get this energy.

How Birds Fly

Each kind of bird has its own pattern of flight. Some birds jump before they take off. Some rise straight up, then glide along without flapping their wings. Some, like the hummingbird, flap their wings rapidly. The large birds of prey soar high and move their wings slowly.

The shape of the wings and the tail feathers indicates the kind of flying a bird does. For example, a white-crowned sparrow (seen in this picture) has short, rounded wings that are good for short, quick flight in its daily movements. A swallow has long, pointed wings and can fly very rapidly.

A bird takes off with the aid of its elevator muscle, located below the level of the wing over the breastbone. A tendon acts like a pulley and pulls the muscle which, in turn, lifts the wing. When the wing moves downward, it does so by means of a large depressor muscle, because the bird needs more strength to move forward by its downward stroke, and to overcome air resistance.

The wing feathers help the bird as it glides. They are strong and separate slightly to allow air to pass through as the bird rises, or they remain together to keep air out on the downstroke.

Some birds spend much of their time flying. When fall approaches, all migratory birds must be in good condition for the difficult journey to their winter territory. They have accumulated fat deposits which help supply energy. They have a newly formed set of feathers for the flight.

66

Birds, Our Fine-feathered Friends

Birds are the only animals with feathers. The feathers keep them warm and dry and are necessary for flight.

Bird feathers are of different sizes. Close to the body is a layer of soft fluffy down. Then there are short, contour feathers that overlap to keep out the rain and keep in the warmth. Each feather is attached by a short stiff quill. It is hollow at the base and quite tranparent. On the shaft are small barbs, flexible but firm.

The feathers streamline a bird and as the bird flies, air passes over them without resistance. When a bird preens himself, he is rubbing drops of oil from a gland at the base of his tail and spreading the oil over his feathers for waterproofing.

The bright colors in bird feathers are sometimes caused by pigment in the feathers. Often they may come from the microscopic prisms which break up daylight into separate colors.

From this painting of a grasshopper sparrow, try to find the short, soft contour feathers of the head, neck, breast and throat. The wing feathers are longer and stiffer and the tail feathers are sometimes the longest, varying in size and shape according to the bird's flying habits.

The painting is by John James Audubon, a pioneer American naturalist who lived from 1785 to 1851. Audubon devoted his lifetime to studying the world of nature. He tried to express what he learned in pictures. His paintings and sketches are still available, showing the structure, colors, and natural environment of birds and mammals as he saw them.

Where Are the Birds in Winter?

Birds do not need a calendar to tell them when summer is ending. When their young have grown and they have filled up on plenty of food and have completed molting, many birds seem to sense that they must move on to warmer regions. At one time people believed that birds went to sleep for the winter. Now we have learned from watching and banding birds and comparing notes with bird-watchers around the world that some birds migrate.

Bird migration is one of the mysteries of nature. Birds fly southward for the winter to a climate that is sometimes not much warmer than where they nest. They migrate to regions where food is plentiful in winter. The birds seem to know just when to start their migration, what route to follow, where to stop, and where to settle. After months of resting and feeding, they get the feeling that it is time to make the return flight to their summer nesting place.

Tree swallows are a familiar sight at dusk in some regions. In late summer they gather in large flocks and start their migration together. They fly only by day and travel as far south as the northern parts of South America. Other birds fly to more southern parts of South America, sometimes a distance of six thousand miles.

Migrating birds have been seen to follow four main flyways. Birds from farthest north start first, join others of their kind and appear to follow one of these paths: (1) along the Atlantic coast to Florida and on to Central or South America; (2) along the valley of the Mississippi and Missouri rivers to the Gulf states; (3) over the Rocky Mountains to Mexico; and (4) along the Pacific coastline to Mexico.

Overwintering Birds

Some birds do not migrate at all. They are the permanent residents in farm regions and the more hardy species in the temperate areas. English sparrows, goldfinches, and quail are some permanent residents that find nourishment during the winter from berries, seeds and other food all about them.

Some overwintering birds in the northern states and in sections where winters are mild are migrants from Canada and the northern parts of New England. The junco is a winter resident, but he really nests and breeds among the fir trees of northern woods. One type of eastern junco, the Carolina junco, migrates in a vertical direction for the winter. He flies only about twelve miles, but one thousand feet in altitude, from the mountain tops to the warmer valleys below.

Juncos are related to sparrows. Those that live east of the Great Plains are the slate-colored juncos. They are gray and white with a flesh-colored beak. The Oregon juncos that live in the western states are chestnut-backed and pink-sided. They are the ones seen in the picture.

Overwintering birds feed on seeds of weeds and grasses, including ragweed and crabgrass. They also look for the berries of shrubs, such as poison ivy and sumac, because these berries stick to the plants over the winter.

People can help feed the birds in winter by placing a regular supply of food in some kind of shelter against snow and rain. Good winter foods for birds are suet, peanut butter and pumpkin or other seeds.

Birds That Live in the Fields: The Meadowlark

Birds that live in the open fields are adapted to that kind of life and they would not survive anywhere else. If the field should be covered up by concrete or submerged by a flood, field birds would leave in search of another field not already populated by birds of their species. They could not live in a forest or near a stream.

The meadowlark is a typical field bird. It is found throughout the United States and Canada. East of the Great Plains lives the eastern meadowlark and in the West is the more melodious western meadowlark. Kansas, Montana, Nebraska, Oregon and Wyoming have chosen this latter as their state bird.

The meadowlark is a member of the blackbird family and a little larger in size than the robin. It is named for its sweet song, but it is not really a lark. The colors blend with the grasses; a brown and yellow body with a black V on the breast. The breast and the throat are yellow, the outer tail feathers white and the wings a light brown. The bird has a low forehead and a long pointed beak.

The nest of the meadowlark is a flimsy, camouflaged shelter of grass, nestled in a clump of tall grass. An overhanging dome gives added protection against rain for the helpless babies within.

The meadowlark feeds on some grains but mostly on insects, such as grasshoppers, crickets, beetles, ants and caterpillars.

The Sparrows

Among the most numerous birds of the United States are the sparrows. There are about 36 different kinds and most have small, gray or brown bodies. Sparrows seem to be able to live in most environments and especially in open fields. The familiar city bird, the English sparrow, is not a sparrow but a weaver finch that was brought over from England.

The bird in this picture is the white-crowned sparrow, a songbird that lives in the United States and Canada. He feeds on large numbers of seeds in spring and fall and on insects in summer. Sparrows are useful birds because they consume a great many weed seeds.

Birds are good parents. The mother bird fashions a nest in which to lay her eggs. Each kind of bird seems to know by instinct where and how to build a nest. The eggs must be kept warm and the mother bird incubates them until they hatch. Young sparrows, like other songbirds, are born naked and blind. They need the warmth and protection of the mother until their feathers grow. Baby birds are usually seen with their mouths wide open. Usually both parents are kept busy bringing them food.

Bird parents are always on guard. The mother usually scolds, chirps loudly and flutters her wings at strange sounds. She stays close to the young until they know how to fly and how to find food.

A nest is a nursery, not a home. When the birds are fully grown, it is usually abandoned. Some kinds of birds, such as the song sparrows, may raise two or three broods a season in the same nest; but each year, and often for each brood, a new nest is built.

73

The Barn Swallow

When we look for birds of the open fields, we soon realize that somewhere near the fields are farms with houses and barns. Some birds have learned to nest among the hustle and bustle of human activity. Do they sense that people will not harm them? Actually, the people are less of a menace than their cats and dogs.

The barn swallow is a field bird that feeds only on insects which it catches in mid-air. It is a small bird, noted for its long, pointed wings and forked tail. These help the bird to rise high and fly swiftly in search of insect food. Swallows also depend on their rapid flight to elude the hawks and other birds of prey. They fly during the day on their migration to South America.

The nest of the barn swallow is usually attached with mud to the beams of barns and other buildings. There are about four young birds in one brood, and the mother is kept busy feeding them. As soon as one brood flies away, the mother gets the nest ready for a second one. There may be a colony of 50 pairs of swallows in a single building.

The barn swallow ranges over most of the United States and almost everywhere in parts of Canada and Alaska. It migrates to Colombia and Central Argentina, in South America.

The Bluebird

One of the loveliest little song birds of the field is the bluebird. Birds have a music-making organ in the throat. It is a cavity with elastic sides that stretch and shrink with the aid of muscles. The muscles determine the speed at which the elastic walls vibrate and thus control the sound.

Birds sing mostly in the spring or at mating season. The males are the singers. They probably sing to warn away other males, to attract a mate, or to show the limits of their territory. Each species of bird has its own call notes. In late summer the bird songs become less frequent. Birds rarely sing in their winter homes in warmer climates.

The bluebird has a red breast. Its back is a vivid blue. It is much smaller than the robin, but like him it belongs to the thrush family. Bluebirds feed on beetles, caterpillars, grasshoppers and on berries. They have learned to live and breed near people since many of their natural nesting sites have disappeared.

Bluebirds nest in cavities of trees but they will also use man-made bird houses. If you want to attract bluebirds, here is the kind of house you might build for them. It should be about ten inches deep and six inches in height and width. The doorway should be about one-and-a-half inches in diameter, to keep out starlings. There should be no threshold. Place the box on a pole in the sun, facing south or east, and about four to eight feet from the ground. The birds may raise two or three broods in it in a single season.

The Eastern Kingbird

The kingbird is a fighter for his rights and makes himself seen and heard when his nest or his feeding territory appears to be in danger.

The eastern kingbird, shown here, is found east of the Rocky Mountains. His nest is built in the open, on a fence post, or in an apple tree. He is about the size of a robin, with a dark back and a light breast. He is large-headed, short-necked and broad-shouldered. There is a distinctive white band across the end of his tail. When excited he sometimes shows his crest of red feathers.

The kingbird is usually seen perched on a treetop or wire, high over the fields, looking for food and guarding his territory. If a larger bird should trespass, he swoops down quickly and cries out loudly to scare the bird away. He seems to enjoy pursuing birds that are larger than himself, uttering a high-pitched battle cry. He chases crows and hawks very skillfully. The size or strength of the other birds does not frighten him. He maneuvers by flying quickly and dashingly wildly around the bird in order to confuse him. After a duel with a crow, for example, it is usually the crow that seeks shelter in a nearby woods.

Kingbirds feed on flying insects, such as grasshoppers, flies and honeybees and on the fruits of many shrubs. They range from New Brunswick, Manitoba and British Columbia to Florida and the Gulf Coast and westward to New Mexico, Utah and western Oregon.

The Killdeer

The killdeer is a slender, slim-legged plover about ten inches in length. It is brown with white underparts and has two black bands across the breast. The killdeer lives in fields throughout most of the United States and Canada.

Killdeer are usually seen in pairs. The female makes a simple nest by scratching a hollow in the ground and lining it with small stones. Here she lays four eggs, each a speckled cream- and chocolate color. She incubates the eggs until they hatch. Young killdeer are quite lively after birth. Their bodies are covered with down and they are soon able to find food for themselves. Although they do not need the long period of feeding and care of young songbirds, young killdeer are protected by the mother until they can fly.

In winter, killdeer migrate to the southern half of the United States or to the northern parts of South America.

The feet of birds tell a great deal about their way of living. The feet of the killdeer are shaped for living on the ground. The front toes are spread out and the hind ones are short. Killdeer can run very rapidly. Some ground birds live by scratching, such as chickens, grouse and quail. Birds that perch on trees or on fences have long, slender toes that grip the perch tightly. Usually three toes point forward and one behind. Birds that live in the water have a web of skin between the front toes.

Gamebirds of the Field: The Bob-white Quail

The bob-white quail is hunted in the fields as game. Unlike the prairie chickens, whose numbers were reduced when the wild prairies were put under cultivation, quail have been able to thrive in the wheat and corn fields of the southernmost states east of the Mississippi River. They are not found in New England.

The pair in the picture illustrate what a small, plump species of bird the quail is. The female is on the left. The bob-white quail gets its name from the "bob-white" call by which it can be recognized. Its coloring is dull buff or black with white stripes and it blends readily into its background. The California quail has a military-looking top-knot of feathers sticking out of its head.

Quail families sometimes remain in their nesting area over the winter. They sleep in a circle, faces turned outward and tails touching. If one bird hears danger, it gives a signal. The whole covey then takes off at once in all directions.

With scant food supply, quail families often perish in the winter. A planting of fencerows, such as multiflora rose or blackberry, will assure these birds protection and a source of food in times of scarcity.

Quail feed on insects and weed seeds. They eat grasshoppers, beetles, weevils, spiders and seeds of ragweed, corn, wheat and poison ivy.

The Ring-necked Pheasant

One of the most beautiful game birds is an import from China. It is the ring-necked pheasant, found in good supply in the fertile fields of the northern parts of the United States.

The male pheasant is unusually colorful and is highly sought as a game bird. He has a green head, bright red spots on his cheeks and a multicolored body with feathers of gold, copper, black and iridescent brown. His tail is long and trailing, sometimes leaving a telltale track in the snow. The pheasant measures more than two feet from head to tip of tail. He has a harsh, two-note cackle of alarm, and like a rooster, he flaps his wings and crows.

Pheasants thrive on farms where there is plenty of cover. Shrubs and cornstalks provide such cover, as do the edges of strips where the farmer has planted row crops.

Pheasants consume large numbers of insects and their larvae, among them grasshoppers, crickets and ants. The weeds that sprout in the fields after harvest time mean much more to these birds than to man. Pigweed, ragweed and tumbleweed seeds keep pheasants, quail and songbirds supplied during the winter. The birds also feed on waste grain and corn left on the ground in the fields.

On a good farm there are enough pheasants to allow a surplus for the farmer's hunting pleasure. Most of those taken are the males, and since there may be several females for each male, the pheasant population can survive after a regulated hunting season.

A Mother Pheasant and Her Brood

The female pheasant, like the female of most animals, has soft quiet colors that blend with the background. In summer she is usually busy brooding or protecting her young.

The pheasant makes a depression in the ground and lines it with grass and leaves. In June she lays a large number of eggs. This is typical of most game birds for the dangers are great and with a large family of chicks, only a few can hope to survive. The eggs are pale brown and they hatch out after three weeks of incubation. Young pheasants, as those shown in the upper picture, are covered with fluffy feathers. They are lively and are able to run about soon after birth.

Mother and chicks leave the nest as soon as the young can follow. They never return to the nest but seek shelter in the shrubs. Together they hunt for insect and plant food. Mother pheasant does not need to carry food to her young, but until they can fly off on their own, she still has to keep them warm and safe from attackers.

Threshing machines that cut an early crop may destroy a covey of young pheasants, quail, or meadowlarks. Some farmers attach flushing bars to the machinery, giving the birds enough warning to fly off before the blades strike. If a pheasant's eggs are destroyed, the parents may start a new nest.

Birds of Prey: Hawks

Hawks, owls, eagles, and vultures are flesh-eaters and so they are "birds of prey." Contrary to previous belief, birds of prey are now recognized as useful, because they tend to keep a check on the wildlife population of the woods and fields. Their food is usually chosen from animals and insects that can multiply beyond the limit of usefulness. These birds often pick off the weakest animals and the ones that survive and multiply are the strongest of their species.

Birds of prey or predators feed on animals in proportion to their size. The hawks that soar over the fields, usually the "mouse hawks," are important in keeping down the supply of rodents. The red-tailed hawk in the picture is perched on a stump to feed on his catch, a mouse. He is one of the larger hawks, measuring about two feet in length with a wingspread of nearly six feet. He has a rounded, unbanded tail.

A small hawk of the fields, about the size of a robin, is the sparrow hawk. This beautifully colored bird has been misnamed. He does not often feed on sparrows but on insects, especially grasshoppers, which are much more suited to his small size.

Hawks hatch a small number of young. Their chicks are born quite helpless and remain in the nest for some time.

Hawks are now protected in most states, because they have been found useful in keeping rats and mice in check. The individual birds that occasionally eat farm animals may be eliminated, but it is no longer considered sportsmanlike to shoot any hawk that comes into sight.

Owls

Owls are important birds of the field and forest. They usually hunt for their animal food under cover of darkness. To help them see in poor light, they have large pupils. The eyes are large and appear even larger because of the border of feathers around them.

Owls are easily distinguished from other birds by a large head, forward-directed eyes and short neck. Some of them have feather "horns" or protruding ear tufts. The short-eared owl in the picture has small tufts, as compared with another species that he resembles, the great horned owl. Owls vary in size. The screech owl, for example, is medium sized, about the size of a robin; the great horned owl is two feet long.

Owls feed on mice, other small mammals and on insects. Their hooked, curved beak is well suited to grasping a small animal quickly. Their movements are noiseless as they approach their prey. When they have finished digesting the food, they cough up waste in the form of small, round pellets. The pellets are clean and odorless, made up of bits of undigested fur and bones. If you pick up these pellets and examine them, you will find out what an owl has been eating.

The short-eared owl lives in open fields and feeds during the day. He is about ten inches long and of a speckled gray and white color. He is often found where there is an oversupply of mice.

Owls are useful birds of prey. They have been needlessly shot down in the past by hunters who considered them a menace to poultry and game birds.

Sanitation Crew of the Fields

Turkey vultures are among the scavengers that usually feed only on dead animals. Scavengers are valuable, because they can quickly dispose of carcasses that would otherwise be left to spread foul odors and disease over the countryside.

The red bare head distinguishes the turkey vulture from other birds of prey. He is about the size of a small domestic turkey, though a fraction of the weight, with a wingspread of nearly six feet. Notice the outspread wings of the bird in the picture. Here is the typical position of the wings in flight: the thicker, black wings forward and the gray flight feathers that extend backward.

Turkey vultures roost in a group of trees; but each morning after the sun is well up they set forth independently to hunt for food. They soar and circle within the thermals, which are rising columns of air warmed and set in motion by the sun. These currents enable the vultures to glide high and far. Turkey vultures have the keen vision of birds of prey. When one bird zooms down to start his meal, others seem to observe him, and soon there is a crew at work.

The vultures range over farm and ranch lands from coast to coast and from southern Canada to the southern tip of South America. In southern United States they are accompanied by the black vulture, a heavier bird with a black head. In flight this bird flaps his wings frequently, while the turkey vulture soars smoothly with few strokes.

CHAPTER V

Mammals: Warm-blooded Animals with Hair

Everyone has seen a mammal, but he may not have known it by that name. Mammals are the most highly developed and the most intelligent of animals. Dogs, cats, cows, and sheep are common mammals. People, too, are mammals.

Mammals are warm-blooded and have hair. The name mammal is derived from the fact that these animals nurse their young with milk secreted in the mammary glands. Most mammals give birth to live young. At some stage in their lives they usually have a furry or hairy covering.

Mammals live in the field, in our backyard, in the forest and jungle, and in the desert. Bats are mammals that live in the air, and whales are mammals that live in the sea.

The mammals shown on the following pages are typical of those that live in fields. First, the plant-eaters are discussed, then some of the flesh-eaters. These are the fewest in number, for among all the mammals most are plant-eaters.

Feeding Time for Meadow Mice

Meadow mice are among the most prolific of mammals. They bear large litters of about five babies each several times a year. A female mouse occasionally starts to breed when she is only a month old.

The young mice in the picture are safely settled in their soft nest of grass, hidden among tall grasses. Their first food is the milk produced in the mother's body. Nursing mother-mice need a great deal of food. They feed on large quantities of wild and cultivated grasses, on bark and roots and on grasshoppers, crickets and other insects.

Meadow mice are one of the most numerous of all mammals, living in all parts of North America. They have small bodies, short legs and soft fur.

They are about six inches long, of which two inches is tail. The color of these mice varies somewhat with the climate and the environment in which they live but generally they are gray and hard to see among the grasses.

From a meadow mouse's nest there are tunnels in the grass that lead up and down the length of the field. About 20 mice live in an acre of good grassland. When their numbers are allowed to increase beyond the normal amount, they do damage to crops.

Fortunately, many animals depend on meadow mice for food. Hawks, owls, foxes, coyotes and snakes are some of them. When enough of these animals are in the fields, meadow mice never become too troublesome.

The Thirteen-lined Ground Squirrel

A few squirrels live in trees and wooded areas. Many species, such as the thirteen-lined squirrel and the Franklin's ground squirrel, live among the grasses in plains and prairie country.

The thirteen-lined squirrel is a small animal with large claws. It has thirteen white or buff stripes, some broken into "stars" against the dark brown back. Its den is an underground burrow. When the squirrel comes out, it tends to sit erect, propped by its tail and looking like a statue.

These squirrels make a bird-like sound as they dart in and out of their burrows. They go into hibernation in October for the winter, emerging in April. Thus they spend about half their time sleeping. The female bears from seven to ten young. They are blind and helpless at birth, like many other mammals.

The thirteen-lined ground squirrels feed on grasses, seeds, insects and occasionally ground-nesting birds. They, in turn, are preyed upon by hawks and flesh-eating mammals, such as badgers and ferrets.

Prairie dogs, a kind of ground squirrel, once swarmed over the prairie lands from North Dakota to Texas. They were so abundant that they had to be controlled when the farmers moved in. At one time, it was estimated that about 800 million prairie dogs lived in Texas, feeding on the grasses that would supply three million head of cattle. Today they are rare and live in scattered colonies, hunted by hawks, owls and coyotes.

The Woodchuck

The woodchuck, also called a marmot, is related to the gnawing mammals of the squirrel family. His popular name is ground hog, said to be derived from the Indian name for this animal, meaning "the diggers." Woodchucks dig into the ground and excavate a chamber. They may burrow under a thicket of brush or hedge. A system of tunnels gives several entrances and exits to the burrow for protection.

The woodchuck in the picture is sniffing the spring air. He is quite thin, probably because his body has used up the stored fat during his winter rest. An Old World legend, once applied to the European badger, has now been transferred to the woodchuck. Each year, it tells, on February 2, the ground hog comes out of his burrow. This is Ground Hog Day. If it is a sunny day and he sees his shadow, he is said to go back for six more weeks of sleep. If it is a rainy or cloudy day, and there is no shadow, he is supposed to sense an early end of winter.

The woodchuck lives in sections of nearly all Canadian provinces and in most sections of northeastern United States. He is a grizzled brown, with darker forepaws and lower legs. The yellow-bellied marmot that inhabits the northwestern regions is larger and lighter in color.

Woodchucks seem always to be feeding. They come out in early morning and late afternoon to feed on clover, weeds (including ragweed) and some green vegetables. In the spring the females need plenty of nourishment because they are nursing mothers. Later in the summer, when the young have grown, the woodchucks begin to fatten themselves for winter hibernation. They may weigh as much as ten pounds by the time fall comes along.

The Pocket Gopher: An Underground Worker

This burrowing rodent is called the pocket gopher. Its range does not extend into the eastern states, but rather in the western parts of North America and the Mississippi Valley, as far south as the Gulf of Mexico. The French word "goupe" means honeycomb, and the gopher is named for its honeycomb arrangement of tunnels that lead to and from its nest.

The pocket gopher spends most of its life underground. It is a powerful digger and has been known to dig a tunnel 250 feet long in a single night. Its long, sharp front claws are used for digging.

This animal is the color of the ground around it, ranging from a pale gray to a very dark brown. It is about ten inches long, with a heavy, thick body, a broad, flattened head and a short neck. Although the tunnel is dark, the gopher moves quickly about in search of food, aided by sensitive "whiskers" in front and a naked little tail in back.

On either side of the mouth the pocket gopher has two fur-lined pouches that extend to its shoulders. These are storage pockets, into which the animal stuffs a supply of food and building materials to be carried to the storehouse. The food consists of roots, bulbs and tubers. When there are many of these animals, they cause damage to crops.

Gophers help to aerate the soil as they move about. The tunnels are useful as waterways through which rain water seeps. Badgers, weasels and snakes feed on gophers.

The Cottontail Rabbit

Rabbits are plant-eaters that get over the ground by hops and leaps. Cottontails live throughout most of the United States and southern Canada. They are vegetarians and feed on various grasses, clover, alfalfa, twigs, bark and sometimes garden vegetables.

Cottontails are about fourteen inches long, of which two inches is the stubby white powder-puff tail. They are gray-brown in color. They have short legs, their hind legs longer than the front ones and serving as an aid in leaping. Their ears are at rest on the neck, but at a sound, the rabbit gets up on its haunches, with ears erect, as you see in the picture.

The split upper lip and the nostrils of rabbits are usually twitching. The split in the lip allows the free use of the upper teeth in cutting the grasses.

Mating season is usually from January to September, and a female may bear four or five families each year. In fact, where the climate is mild — in southern and Pacific regions — rabbits may breed at any time throughout the year after rainy weather. The rabbit's nest is an excavation about three inches deep, lined with grass and fur. Many of the young rabbits fall prey to foxes, hawks, owls, snakes and cats.

Rabbits do not hibernate. In the winter they feed on the bark and twigs of young trees. Their footprints are a familiar mark in the soft winter snow.

The Jack Rabbit

The jack rabbit is a long-legged, long-eared animal. It can leap as high as 15 feet if necessary. To escape danger, it has been known to run about 35 miles an hour in great easy bounds. But in its ordinary food-getting movements, the jack rabbit does not leap so high nor run so fast.

In the picture is a black-tailed jack rabbit, named for a streak of black on the lower part of the tail. It is grayish or gray-brown in color. This species of jack rabbit lives in western United States, north to southwestern Oregon, eastward to Nebraska, and south to Mexico. It lives in dry, open country.

The jack rabbit is a vegetarian, feeding on grasses and seeds in season and on the twigs and bark of young trees in winter. Each female jack rabbit may have about four broods a year, though there may not be many in a single litter.

The jack rabbit was introduced into Oregon. So well has it become established there, that a recent count showed some 20 million in half the state. When the animals are numerous, they can damage farmlands. Coyotes, wolves, foxes and other predators help to keep their number in check.

The snowshoe rabbit inhabits northern North America, south to the mountains of Virginia, and west to New Mexico and California. It tends to take on a white fur in winter.

Round-up Time on the Range

Among the largest of the plant-eating mammals are the hoofed browsers, including cows, sheep and horses. Vast numbers of these animals are needed to keep our people fed.

In the wide open spaces of the western mountain states and provinces, beef cattle are allowed to feed in open grassland. As they use up the food in one range, the cowboys round them up and take them to another range. Grazing cattle can keep a field in excellent condition. As they move from plant to plant, the decay from their droppings helps restore plant nutrients to the soil. As long as the number of cattle stays within the "carrying capacity" of the range, the grasslands will continue to grow.

Some cattle are fed and sheltered against the cold. Among the domesticated kinds are Herefords and Shorthorns, bred for their beef; Holsteins, Guernseys, Jerseys, and Ayrshire are bred for their milk. These cattle are grazed on cultivated grasses in lush farm country and in winter they are fed hay and other plant foods. Their diet is carefully regulated to assure a good quality of milk or beef.

The Skunk, a Plant-eater and a Flesh-eater

Animals that feed on other animals are the *carnivores*. Those that feed on plants are the *herbivores*. Some carnivores, like the skunk, add fruits to their diet in season. Animals that eat equally of animal and plant matter are the *omnivores*.

Carnivorous or flesh-eating mammals belong to five large groups: cats, dogs, bears, raccoons and weasels. Wolves, coyotes and foxes are in the dog group; pumas, jaguars and lynxes are cats. The skunk, one of the weasel members, is seen in most of North America. The striped one, shown here, is the most common species. It is black and white with a soft shiny fur. It has two broad white stripes along the side and some white on the tail. Another species, the hooded skunk, has two stripes of white along the back from neck to tail.

Skunks den in the ground, sometimes in an abandoned woodchuck's burrow. They feed late in the afternoon and at night, and sleep during the day. Their favorite food is insects, such as grasshoppers, crickets and caterpillars. They also feed on toads, frogs, turtle eggs, mice and game birds. In season they will add some berries and other wild fruits to this diet.

The skunk has a great weapon of defense in its odor. The strong-smelling oil is squirted from glands at the base of its tail. So strong is this liquid that it can blind its victim temporarily.

The skunk will first warn the other animal by thumping on the ground, and if the other animal still approaches, the skunk will spray its "poison gas." The glands hold enough liquid for several shots. Armed with this powerful defense, the skunk has few enemies. However, it is one of the foods of the great horned owl.

The Badger, a Burrowing Flesh-eater

The badger is a stocky, flat-bodied animal with a flattened head and short legs and tail. It has long, shaggy fur, of silvery-gray color, grizzled with brown and black. It is a digging animal, and with its large, heavy claws can dig itself a quick getaway in case of danger.

The badger is a fierce animal, and few animals ever attack it. It has powerful jaws, a thick covering of hair, and loose skin. The badger in the picture appears poised to catch a ground squirrel. He watches the opening to the burrow then digs a tunnel straight down to it. He knows how to trap various ground-living rodents that are much swifter than he is. He devours enormous numbers of rodents.

Badgers feed on meat, fresh or carrion. The excess supply is stored underground and dug up as they need it. In winter badgers slow down on their activities and spend much time sleeping, but they do not hibernate.

The range of these animals has shifted as the prairies have disappeared. They are found in the northern and north central states, south to Texas and Mexico, west to California, and north to British Columbia, Saskatchewan, and Alberta.

The Coyote, Prairie Wolf

By its long canine teeth you can recognize the coyote as a flesh-eater. Coyotes and other mammals that feed on mice and rabbits have well-developed canine teeth. These teeth are used to grip the prey and pierce it.

The teeth of mammals are of various shapes and sizes. Each kind of mammal has specially developed teeth that help it in its food-getting. For example, the dogs have large canine teeth. The grass-eating grazers, the cows, have large molars. Gnawing mammals, like squirrels, have large incisors or cutting teeth.

The coyote is a small wolf that lives in the prairies and plains and in some woodlands of Ontario, western United States, and in some states east of the Mississippi. It is a graceful, dog-like animal, with a shaggy coat of grizzled gray and with a black-tipped tail. It roams by day as well as at night in search of mice, jack rabbits, gophers and snakes. A variety of vegetable matter is also consumed. Its distinctive howl resounds through the quiet night.

The coyote's keen sense of smell sometimes leads him to a sheep pasture. At one time farmers and hunters outlawed coyotes as a menace to all farm animals. But as the supply of coyotes decreased, the population of mice was seen to increase, and damage to crops was great. By allowing the coyotes to roam the meadows and prairies, farmers let nature keep the rodent population in check.

The Red Fox

Mammals that are related to dogs appear to have a high degree of intelligence. The red fox, sly Renard of Aesop's Fables, even looks intelligent. He can wag his bushy tail and bark. When he is aroused he has an expressive growl.

A fox has various ways of eluding domestic dogs. He will run quickly over a dry path that does not pick up his scent. Then he will retrace his steps to confuse the hunter's dogs. Or a fox will hide among cattle and sheep where his scent is lost. Although these and many other tales of a fox's cunning are questionable, there is no denying that the fox is skillful in getting away from his enemy, the dog.

Red foxes live in most regions of the United States and Canada, except in the southern states and on the Pa-

cific coast. They den in a hole in open fields or woods, or in an abandoned burrow of a woodchuck. They feed on mice, rabbits, snakes, frogs, birds, insects and wild fruits or berries in season.

Foxes, like dogs and cats, are devoted parents. As young pups are exposed to attack from coyotes, wolves, and bobcats, the parents remain close by. Both parents join in the hunt for food for their young.

The young foxes in the picture are red, with black ears and white-tipped, bushy tails. In some litters there may be a few red foxes, one black fox, one silver fox, and one "cross" fox that has a black and red body. Silver foxes are raised for the fur trade on fox farms.

Foxes are usually welcome predators where mice abound and where poultry is safely penned.

CHAPTER VI

The Community of Living Things

These, then, are some of the plants and animals of the fields and vast prairies. They are part of the community of living things in open or non-forested lands. They are all part of a large pattern, in which each depends on the other.

The animals thrive where they can find food, water, and good cover or places to rear their young. The plants are limited by the amount of moisture and the available minerals in the soil. None of them can change the environment to suit its own needs. Man alone can do this.

Man can adapt himself to almost any kind of environment. If he lives in a dry land, he can dig for water, or can transport it to keep himself and his crops supplied with water. On marshy land he can grow crops by draining off the water. In a hot season, he can reduce the temperature in his home. In winter, he knows how to keep himself warm.

Unfortunately, as man has changed his environment, he has caused a great loss to the soil, and to plants and animals that existed there. In this chapter are scenes of man's use and abuse of the land; and of man's increasing attempts to control and use the natural bounty that he has inherited.

A Field Community

These are the plants and animals of the field. We are seeing them "at home" in their natural habitat. The study of living plants and animals in their natural setting is called ecology (from the Greek word, *ecos,* meaning home). Through the study of ecology, we learn how each plant and animal gets along in its natural community of living things. We see how it depends on the presence of other plants and animals that live in the same area. We learn what conditions of soil, water and temperature are best suited to the plants and animals living in the same area.

A complicated network of interrelationships exists in a wildlife community. One animal feeds on another which in turn feeds on still another which feeds on a plant. Such feeding relationships are called food chains. Each plant or animal in a chain comprises one "link." There are other relationships, too. For example, red clover is a good animal food and soil fertilizer. It is pollinated with the help of long-tongued bumblebees. Bumblebees nest and multiply in the nests of meadow mice. The farmer understands, therefore, that with a normal population of mice, there will be an adequate number of bees and, in turn, a good supply of red clover. Do you see any food chains in the picture?

Land management workers study the ways of plants and animals and guide farmers in working toward a natural balance. They have noted that where there is a good natural environment, there is a good supply of wildlife. If there is too little food and cover, and too many animals, some animals will perish. Only those will survive for which the field can provide adequate food and cover.

Fields in Balance

These fields have good cover to hold down the soil and protect it against erosion by wind and water. Decaying plant and animal matter are gradually increasing the fertility of the soil, making it possible for more plants to grow. In such fields live many birds, insects, and mammals.

Such land must help to produce most of the food and clothing for the people of our nation and for those to follow in generations to come. Only one-fourth of the two billion acres in the United States is cultivated; one-third is used for grazing; about one-third is forested timberland. We might appraise our land resources by these figures: there are about three acres of cultivated land per person in the United States; about a fiftieth of an acre per person in China; a thirty-eighth of an acre per person in Great Britain; and a twentieth of an acre per person in Japan.

We must, however, conserve our fertile land. Workers in land-use management are helping farmers to get the best quality and the largest quantity of crops with the least amount of loss to the soil.

This means making good use of hillsides and sloping land. It means selecting the proper crops for the soil, and rotating them to keep the soil fertile. It means planting trees as windbreaks, and shrubs as cover for wildlife along the margins of the fields.

Green fields and the many kinds of animals they shelter are a beautiful picture and a source of pleasure to everyone who knows how to read the story they tell of healthy land.

A Field Out of Balance

This was once a farm where people were housed, clothed and fed from the plants and livestock that grew there. The farmer's heritage from millions of years of soil-building has "gone with the wind." Not only has the topsoil disappeared, but with it went the water supply, the wildlife, the farm animals and — the people.

The soil of this region was suitable for grazing and for a limited kind of farming. Such soil exists in Oklahoma, Kansas, Nebraska and parts of Texas. The farmers planted corn and wheat because the market price was high. Year after year, through lack of understanding, these farmers continued to raise the same crop — wheat and corn. The soil nutrients, especially the nitrogen, became exhausted and the soil became dry, loose and barren.

Scenes like this one stretch many miles, and the danger of more wind erosion continues. When strong winds move over bare land, the topsoil is carried with it, leaving only the subsoil exposed. Where once there were crops, there is now only hard subsoil. Where once rabbits, meadow larks and other animals abounded, there is now stillness and wasteland.

This land can be restored to productivity. A farmer with a long-range plan can try once more. With the aid of agricultural experts he can plan to grow a kind of cover grass that will begin to hold the soil in place. After a few seasons, he will turn under the crop for fertilizer or "green manure." A feeding of commercial fertilizer will hasten the soil-building process. Then when the soil is suitable, he will raise only crops that will conserve the good topsoil. For nature to restore the productivity of the land would take several hundred years. Man, by careful planning, can greatly hasten the process, but it will still take a long time.

Gullies Where Crops Once Grew

Scenes like this one are all too frequent in many sections of the United States. Fertile soil has been washed downhill by strong rains because of up-and-down farming on land that sloped.

These gullies were washed out as you might make gullies at the beach, by pouring pails of water over the sand. Heavy rains carry tons of fertile soil through ever-widening and ever-deepening waterways. Many of the gullies are deep enough for a man to stand in, and some may be up to a hundred feet deep. This eroded barren land may extend for miles, land that should be yielding crops.

What of the soil that was carried downhill? It has been washed into surrounding streams and rivers, muddying the clear waters and suffocating the insect and plant life that fish need. Other times the mud is deposited on top of fertile fields, destroying the crops growing in them.

Hillsides are a special problem to a farmer. He must plow in contours or on terraces to avoid water runoff. He must plan his crops to have some growth during all seasons of the year. On most land, minerals are lost by leaching, the water falling on porous soil and seeping down, dissolving the plant nutrients and carrying them deeper into the soil, beyond the reach of the roots.

Gullies can be stopped and reclaimed. The lower picture was taken about three years after the planting of black locust trees. These are fast-growing trees, and as they grow, they enrich the soil and allow cover grasses to take root. This land may never be restored to its original fertility, but it will help to absorb the rain water and further erosion will be reduced.

A Patchwork of Fertile Fields

The view from an airliner over much of the farmlands of the nation is a patchwork of design and color. It is almost as though the farmers were putting on a huge pageant for the benefit of the air passengers.

This pattern of fertile fields is a symbol of the design for living which makes up the landscape. It is a design for a better life now and in the future. The fertile fields of this Minnesota prairie extend for many miles around.

On this July day, we can note the distinctive patterns made by contour plowing. The dotted gray strips are wheat fields that have already been harvested. Shocks of hay left to dry in the sun and the edges of the strips contain food for pheasants, quail, meadowlarks and many mammals. On the white sections in the background are fields of wheat that have not been cut. On the dark silt loam strips are fresh plantings of crops that will mature in the fall.

By such "staggered plantings" and by contour plowings, heavy rains fall upon a waiting sponge, the ground absorbing the water slowly, and allowing it to seep down to the ground water table. The harvested crop residue is left to decay on the ground. The roots hold down the soil and the stubble, later, will add to the humus.

The Rotation of Crops

The best way to conserve the food substances that plants need is to follow the natural method. When a farmer harvests a crop, he notices that new plants begin to grow immediately. It may be ragweed that sprouts in a harvested field. This plant, though unpopular, is of great value to the soil because it binds the topsoil against strong winter winds. When it decays, it restores some of the nutrients that were used up when the wheat plants grew. Ragweed, incidentally, is excellent food for game birds.

But, to maintain a fertile soil, the farmer cannot afford to grow weeds. He must raise marketable crops. By rotating the crops he is helping to keep the soil rich. Here is a sequence of a five-year plan. This farmer plants corn the first year; wheat the second year; a hay crop the third and fourth years; and corn the fifth year. Each crop uses soil nutrients in a different proportion, and as the stubble decays, minerals are restored to the soil. Yet, while the soil is being nourished, the farmer is earning income from the crops.

In rotation of crops, the farmer does not overlook good farming practices, as proper plowing and terracing to prevent water and wind erosion. He also leaves the stubble to decay as a mulch on the ground. Stubble mulching protects the soil in winter and adds a natural form of fertilizer.

Man Against Insects

With modern, large-scale farming have come new problems of insect control. When grasslands grew naturally, there were many varieties of plants where many species of insects lived. These insects competed with one another for food, and each had to forage around for its preferred plant. On the vast stretches of one-crop farms today, the insects find themselves with a huge picnic table on which they are able to feed unchecked.

A field can support a certain number of insects without great damage to the crops, but beyond that number the plants suffer. Each crop has its own insect population, and scientists have been hard at work to find methods of keeping them under control.

Chemical poisons, such as DDT, are the most common form of control. A large area can be sprayed by a tractor-drawn machine, but small planes can cover a field in a small fraction of the

time. DDT and other "super-chemicals" have successfully checked insect invasions. But they must be used with care because too strong a solution may destroy other animals that live in the fields as well as those insects for whose control they were used. These chemicals are also dangerous to man if he comes in contact with excessive amounts. DDT, like arsenic, is stored in the body. Residues on plants may have long-term effects on the animals that consume them for food.

It is recommended by agricultural experts that farmers use sprays in minimum doses recommended for each particular insect. Spraying that is done before the birds hatch their eggs, or at the end of the summer, will not affect young birds in their nests. Care must be taken to keep the spray away from streams because insects and cold-blooded vertebrates which drink this water are especially susceptible to the poison.

"Grass Once Grew There, Too"

A wire fence is all that separates the good grassland from land supporting a crop of annual weeds. Perennial grass once grew outside the fence, too. Both sides of the fence once had the same soil and the same amount of moisture. Yet on one side there is now only dry rocky ground. The difference was caused by overgrazing.

Cattle grazing is a primary use for much of the grassland in the western

states where the soil is unsuited or the rainfall too low for other kinds of farming. Grazing herds help to fertilize the soil with their wastes and spread seed as they move among the plants.

Where too many animals compete for the grass, however, the plants are consumed before they can produce seed. There is a great difference in the number of cattle that can graze on western grasslands and those that can be maintained in a good planted pasture. In some sections, a single cow might need ten acres per month. In good farming country, cattle need a smaller area because their food is more plentiful.

Ranchers have learned that the best grazing practice is to limit the number of head of cattle to the forage *available each year* so that the good plants retain their vigor, reproduce and protect the soil against erosion by wind and water.

The Cattle of Yesteryear

When the American Indians lived in the plains areas, there were millions of bison, or buffaloes. These cattle roamed in herds from the Allegheny to the Sierra Nevada Mountains, and from southern Texas to Canada. They fed on wild grasses and, as they searched for water, they made the first trails used by the white man. The estimated number of buffaloes was once 60 million. Today the only ones alive are those protected on wildlife refuges, such as the National Bison Refuge in Montana, where this buffalo family lives.

The white settlers hunted and slaughtered the buffalo until only a few remained. When after the Civil War, the railroads spread over the land, buffalo skins were shipped in large quantities for robes and clothing. Buf-falo Bill got his nickname for his prowess in hunting buffalo. He killed more than 4,000 of them in 18 months. Thousands of these were slaughtered for their hides and their meat left to rot.

The Texas longhorn cattle, shown in the lower picture, were brought to our country by Spanish settlers in 1521, and they were raised so successfully that they once numbered millions. When the more hardy Brahma cattle were brought into the Southwest, the longhorns began to disappear. Thanks to the efforts of two Forest Service officials — John Hatton and Will C. Barnes — the longhorns were saved from total extinction. About 500 still survive in national wildlife refuges operated by the Fish and Wildlife Service of the U. S. Department of the Interior.

A Haven for Wildlife

Many of the good practices of the farmer have created good habitat for wildlife.

The field shown here is an excellent haven for rabbits, pheasants, skunks and quail. The shocks of hay in the field give additional food and cover. Brush-piles, from pruned branches and hedges between the fields, give added cover for rabbits, skunks and quail.

Wildlife adds charm and beauty to the field. The greater the variety of plants grown, the more kinds of birds and mammals will be found.

Animals are a great aid in keeping down the number of destructive insects and rodents. Whenever too many of a single species appear, its predators increase and enjoy the bountiful supply of food. It has been found that wildlife helps to check the population of destructive insects and mice.

On one farm where skunks were suspected of causing damage to an alfalfa crop, a test was carried out. A small area of the sheep pasture was fenced in by wire to keep out sheep and skunks. At the end of the summer, three-fourths of the hay within the enclosure had been destroyed, not by the skunks, but by mice. The mice had, in fact, eaten more of the hay than the sheep would have eaten. The farmer wisely concluded that it was more important to allow skunks on the land than to let the mice multiply unchecked.

The Hunting Season Is On

About 14 million people each year receive licenses to hunt game birds and mammals. At one time animals were ruthlessly killed, even exterminated. Today, hunting is carried on under conditions that assure the survival of each kind of animal.

Since the days when hunting was a necessity, man has enjoyed this sport. It requires patience, a keen eye, a nimble body, a love of the outdoors and a knowledge of animal ways. Hunting is regulated in all of our states by law. Songbirds, for example, are protected in all states; hawks and owls in some states; quail in a few.

The hunting season is in the fall, after the young animals have matured. Hunters must have a license, and the fees from these licenses — together with the tax on the price of weapons and ammunition — help to maintain departments of conservation in each state. Each agency studies the wildlife in its region, manages state-owned land and enforces game laws. Hunting is done on special preserves or on private property *with the permission of the owner.*

Game animals tend to multiply rapidly. From 28 rabbits in spring, there may be about 74 in the fall. Quail will increase their number by about 700 per cent in a season.

These large populations of animals in the fall cannot survive over the winter. Only a few will survive until the spring. Game animals are considered a "crop" that can be harvested when there is a surplus. Our game laws are adjusted from year to year to assure that only the excess will be shot. It is important that an adequate breeding stock be left at the close of each hunting season every year.

Young Workers for Wildlife

Young people play an active part in wildlife management in those sections where the problem is part of the everyday life.

Shrubs are set out as food and cover for wildlife by the young people in Jasper and Newton Counties, Missouri (upper picture), as part of a cooperative program. The Missouri Conservation Commission, local businessmen and property owners have all joined forces to improve the wildlife habitat of that region.

Members of 4-H clubs play an important part in wildlife and conservation activities. The group's work under the state and local extension services of the United States Department of Agriculture. The team in the lower picture is part of a land-judging contest in Oklahoma, in which a thousand young people took part.

Boy Scouts, Girl Scouts and Camp Fire Girls are pledged to the conservation of natural resources. A Boy Scout Merit Badge is offered for those who complete projects in conservation and wildlife management. Senior Girl Scouts may work with local forestry agents on conservation projects. One of their goals is to help establish local Lou Henry Hoover Forests or Sanctuaries, in honor of the late Mrs. Herbert Hoover who was an active conservationist.

In some communities, as in Gaston County, North Carolina, it is the schools that emphasize conservation education. The students there take field trips to study the natural environment, plant shrubs and provide more food and water for wildlife.

From Knowledge Comes Pleasure

These men and women are exploring the community of living things. They have set aside a square, or quadrat of land, in which to take a census of plant and animal life.

Plants are listed by species, with the number of each within the area, and the dates of their development. Insects are counted by sweep nets, such as the ones in the picture. A ten-inch net is used, and each person counts the number and kinds of insects caught in a hundred sweeps. After a thousand sweeps, insect species not caught in the net are considered absent from this area.

Mammals are counted by the number of burrows in the area, or by a census taken while slowly driving a car over the road. Birds are counted by their nests and by those seen in a walk or ride. They are also counted by the number of singing males within the area.

The study of animals and their habits is endless. Each season brings new thrills, especially when a species new to the area appears unexpectedly. Bird watchers enjoy taking bird counts at different seasons, and keeping lists of birds seen each year. Many keep life lists of birds they have personally identified. Trying to add new species to this life list becomes a sort of game.

From a knowledge of the habits of insects, birds, mammals and plants come many fine hobbies and from such knowledge springs an active interest in the conservation of the natural community and natural resources.

Watching for Wildlife

Childhood hobbies often become adult hobbies. They may even lead to the choice of a vocation. These young bird-watchers are being guided by Roger Tory Peterson,* who started his career as a member of an Audubon Junior Club. His interest in the world of nature became a hobby and his hobby led to further study. Mr. Peterson is a leading ornithologist, author, nature artist and photographer-lecturer.

Tens of thousands of young people are similarly studying the ways of plants and animals. They learn how each species lives, the kind of environment it requires, and how all fit into the larger pattern of a habitat. A study of the habits of insects, snakes, birds and mammals is included in the program of some schools. The various youth organizations, such as Boy Scouts of America, Girl Scouts of America, Campfire Girls, 4-H Clubs and the Audubon Junior Clubs, engage in field and camping trips where wildlife is best studied.

A keen eye uncovers many interesting facts about plants and animals, and bring a richer and more enjoyable use of leisure time. If we begin at school age to explore the outdoors and learn to appreciate the living things around us we will be happier adults and better citizens because we will understand the importance of our natural resources, the soil, water, plants, and wildlife, and the need to use them wisely.

*See Mr. Peterson's Foreword to this book.

Index

A

Air, composition of 12-13
Alfalfa 32-33, 56
Altricial birds 72, 73, *80
Amphibians 17, *60
Anemone, western *27
Animals depend on plants 12-13, 16, 17, 18, 20-21, 30, 31, 36, 47, 58
Animals, flesh-eaters 16, 18, 36, 40, 41, 44, 46, 49, 52, 53, 57, 59, 60, 63, 72, 74, 75, 76, 78, 79, 80, 81, 82, 83, 86, 90, 92, 93, 95, 99
Animals, plant-eaters 16, 17, 18, 31, 46, 53, 70-71, 73, 78, 79, 80, 85, 86, 87, 88, 89, 90, 91, 92
Annelids 58
Ants *53, 72
Aphids *45
Apiary *56
Apple tree 37
Arachnids 59
Asters 28
Audubon
  Junior Clubs 119
  John James 67
Autumn 19

B

Bacteria 12-13, 18, 23, *24
Badger 88, *93
Balance of nature 11, 17, 18, 27, 36, 53, 81, 85, 86, 91, 94
Barberry 36
Barley 34-35
Bee dance 55
Beekeeping 56
Beetles 45, *46, 49, 72, 75, 78
Bird, circulation and digestion of 65
  feeding 70-71
  songs 75
  laws for protection of 81, 82, 83
  structure *65, 66, 77
Birdhouse 75
Birds of the field 17, 18, 19, 27, 32-33, 49, 52
Birds of prey see Prey, birds of
Bison *112-*113
Blackberry 36
Black-eyed susan 28
Blueberry 36
Bluebird *75
Bobolinks 36
Bob-white see Quail

Bryophytes 23
Buffalo Bill 112-113
Buffaloes *112-*113
Bumblebees 27, *54, 97
Butterfly 17, 18
  monarch 19, 30, *47, *48, *49, *50
  swallowtail *51
  trees 50
  viceroy 48

C

Campfire Girls 116-117, 119
Camouflage in nature 41, 72, 78
Canada, animals found in *46, *50, *51, *56, *61, *72, *74, *76, *77, 83, *87, *89, *90, 92, *93, *94, *95, 112-113
Carbon dioxide 12-13, 16
Carnivores see Animals, flesh-eaters
Carrying capacity 11, 91
Catbirds 36
Cattle 32-33, 86, *91, 110-111, *112-*113
Cell structure *24
Cereal plants *34-*35
Chickadees 45
Chlorophyll 16, 19, 23, 24, 26
Cicadas *44
Clouds and water vapor 12-13
Clover, red 18, 24, 27, 32-33, 34-35, 54, 87, 97, *106-*107
Coal from plants 16
Cold-blooded animals 20-21
Coleoptera 46
Color in leaves 19
Conservation, education for 116-117, 119
Contour plowing *34-*35, *104-*105
Corn *34-*35, *106-*107
Counting insects *118
Cowboys *91
Cows for beef and milk *91
Coyotes 85, 90, 92, *94
Crabgrass 18, 70-71
Cricket *43, 72, 85
Crows 60, 76
Cycle of life 16, 17, 18, 19, 20-21, 24, 28

D

Daddy-long-legs 59
Daisies *28
Darwin, Charles 58

Defensive mechanism 92
Dispersal, plant 27, 28, *30, 37
Dogs 94

E

Eagles 63
Early settlers to New World 32-33, 56, 112-113
Earthworms 18, 20-21, 58
Ecology 97 see also Balance of Nature
Elements in soil 14-15
Elm 37
Energy in plants 16
Erosion, soil 34-35, *102-*103

F

Fall
Farms 19, *20-*21, *32-*33, *34-*35, *36, 90, *97, *98-*99, *100-*101, *104-*105
Feathers
  Bird 65
  butterfly 51
Fertile soil see Soil
Fertilization see Pollen
Flight of birds 66
Flowers 18, 23, *27, *28, *30
  composite *28
Flycatchers 45
Food chains 97
Forage crops *32-*33, *34-*35, 91
Four-H Clubs 116-117, 119
Foxes 36, 85, 89, 90, *95
Frogs 60 see also Amphibians
Fungi 18, *26

G

Game
  birds *78, *79, *80
  mammals 89, 115
Gaston Co., North Car. 116-117
Goldenrod 28
Goldfinches 36
Gophers, pocket *88, 94
Grasses *32-*33, *34-*35, 85, 91
Grasshoppers *40, *42, 72, 75, 78, 85, 92
Groundhog 87
Ground water 14-15, 17, 37, 104-105
Gullies *102-*103

H

Hares *90
Hatton, John and Barnes,
    Will C. 112-113
Hawks 60, 74, 76, *81, 85,
    89
Hawthorn tree 37
Herbivores see Animals,
    plant-eaters
Hibernation 20-21, 86, 87,
    93
Homoptera 44, 45
Honeybees *55, *56
Hoover, Lou Henry Forests
    116-117
Hummingbirds 52
Humus 14-15, 100-101
Hunting 78, 79, *115
Hymenoptera 53, 54, 55, 57

I

Insects 19, 20-21, 27, 28, 32-
    33, 34-35, 72, 79, 80
Insects, chemical control of
    46, 108-109

J

Jasper Co., Mo. 116-117
Juncos *70-*71

K

Katydids *42
Killdeer *77
Kingbirds *76

L

Leaves 19, 23
Legumes see clover
Lepidoptera 47, 48, 49, 50,
    51, 52
Longhorns, Texas *112-
    *113

M

Mammals 32-33, 34-35, 36
Marmot see Woodchuck
Meadowlarks 17, 36, *72,
    80
Metamorphosis, complete
    47, 48, 49, 51, 52, 53
Metamorphosis,
    incomplete 40, 41
Mice 18, 36, 81, *85, 115
    meadow *85
Migration
    birds 17, 19, 68-69, 74,
        76, 77
    monarch butterfly 50
Milkweed *30, 47

Mimicry in nature 48
Minerals in soil 14-15
Missouri Conservation
    Commission 116-117
Mites 59
Moles 20-21, 26
Moths 18, *52
Mushrooms *26

N

Newton Co., Mo. 116-117
Night-feeding animals see
    katydids, moths, owls,
    toads, coyotes
Nitrogen 12-13, 24, 34-35

O

Oats 34-35
Opossums 63
Orthoptera 40, 41, 42, 43
Ovary 27
Overwintering
    birds *20-*21, *70-*71,
        78, 79, 80
    mammals 89, 90
Owls *82, 89
Oxygen 12-13, 65

P

Parasites 26, 45, 49, 52, 57
Perennial plants 28
Peterson, Roger Tory *119
Pheasants *79, *80, 104-105
Photosynthesis 12-13
Pistil *23, 27
Plant
    processes 12-13, 14-15, 16,
        17, 18, 19, 23, 24, 27, 28
    structure 23, 24, 26, 27,
        28, 30
Plants
    depend on animals 16,
        17, 18, 27, 28
Plover see killdeer
Poison
    ivy *31, 78
    oak 31
    sumac 31
Pollen, transfer of 17, *27,
    28, 49
Pollination see Pollen
Prairie dogs 86
Praying Mantis *41
Precocial birds 77
Predators see Animals,
    flesh-eaters
Prey, birds of *81, *82, *83
Pteridophytes 23

Q

Quail 36, *78, 104-105, 114,
    115

R

Rabbits 18, 36, *89, *90,
    114, 115
Rain water 12-13, 14-15, 17,
    102-103
Reproduction, animal 40,
    41, 42, 43, 44, 45, *47,
    *48, *49, 50, 51, 53, *54,
    55, *57, 58, 60, *63, 77,
    *80, 81, *85, 86, 95, 115
Reproduction, plant *24,
    26, 31, 32-33, 34-35, 36, 37
Reptiles *61
Roadrunner 63
Robins 58
Rodents 18, 85; 86, 87, 88,
    89
Roses, multiflora *36, 78
Rotation of crops 34-35,
    *106-*107
Rye 34-35

S

Sainfoin 32-33
Saprophytes 26
Scavengers *83
Scientific research 23, 24,
    58, 118
Scorpions 59
Scouts, Boy and Girl 116-
    117, 119
Seasons of the year *17,
    *18, *19, *20-*21
Seed dispersal see dispersal,
    plant
Seeds of plants 18, 19, 20-
    21, 23, *27, *30, 78
Sheep *11, 114
Shrubs of the field 17, 19,
    20-21, 31, *36, 70-71, 78,
    80, 116-117
Silk
    from plants *30
    from insects 47, 48, 49, 50,
        51, 52
    from spiders *59
Skunks 26, 60, *92, 114
Snakes 20-21, 59, *62, *63,
    85, 88
Snow *20-*21
Sod 32-33, 34-35, 91
Soil *14-15, 18, 26, 30, 32-
    33, 34-35, 36, 37, 88
Soil erosion see Erosion

Sounds
  bird 75
  insect 42, 43, 44
Sparrow
  English 73
  grasshopper *67
  song 36
  white-crowned *66, *73
Sparrows 73
Spiders 78
  orange garden *59
  black widow 59
Spring season 17
Squirrels 26, *86, 114
Stamen *23, 27
Stigma *23, 27
Sting
  of bee 57
  of spider 59
  of wasp 57
Strip planting *34-*35

Subsoil 14-15
Suiter Fescue grass *32-*33
Sumac 36
Summer 18
Sunflower 28
Sunlight and plants 12-13, 16, 17
Swallows 66, 68-69, *74

T

Tarantula spiders 59
Teeth, animal 62, 94
Thallophytes 23
Ticks 59
Toads 23, 59, *60
Toadstools 26
Topsoil 34-35
Trees of the field 17, 18, 19, 20-21, 34-35, 37, 102-103

Trillium 28
Truk's cap lily 28
Turtles 26, *61

V

Vertebrates 60, *61, *62, 63
Vines 70-71
Von Frisch, Dr. Karl 57
Vultures *83

W

Warm-blooded animals *see* Birds, Mammals
Wasps 17, 44, *57
Water
  for plants 12-13, 17, 104-105
Weasels 88, 92
Wildlife management 114, 115
Woodchuck *87

Picture Acknowledgements

Page 11   Allan D. Cruickshank, National Audubon Society

Page 12-13   Standard Oil Company, New Jersey

Page 14-15   Standard Oil Company, New Jersey

Page 16-17   Jack Dermid, National Audubon Society; John H. Gerard, National Audubon Society

Page 18-19   John H. Gerard, National Audubon Society; Jane Woolridge, National Audubon Society

Page 20-21   American Museum of Natural History

Page 23   Gerhard Ramberg, drawing

Page 24   American Museum of Natural History

Page 26-27   Hugh Spencer, National Audubon Society; John O. Sumner, National Audubon Society

Page 28   Hal H. Harrison, National Audubon Society

Page 30-31   Hal H. Harrison, National Audubon Society; Leonard Lee Rue, National Audubon Society; Hal H. Harrison, National Audubon Society

Page 32-33   Soil Conservation Service, U. S. Department of Agriculture

Page 34-35   Soil Conservation Service, U. S. Department of Agriculture

Page 36-37   Soil Conservation Service, U. S. Department of Agriculture; Standard Oil Company, New Jersey

Page 40-41   Lee Jenkins, National Audubon Society; Howard La Mell, National Audubon Society

Page 42-43   Lynwood M. Chace, National Audubon Society; Hal H. Harrison, National Audubon Society

Page 44-45   Lee Jenkins, National Audubon Society

Page 46-47   Lee Jenkins & Lynwood M. Chace, National Audubon Society; Hugh Spencer & Lee Jenkins, National Audubon Society

Page 48-49   Louis Quitt, National Audubon Society; William J. Jahoda, National Audubon Society

Page 50-51   Hugh M. Halliday, National Audubon Society; Don Wooldridge, National Audubon Society; Lynwood M. Chace, National Audubon Society

Page 52-53   Lynwood M. Chace, National Audubon Society; Hal H. Harrison, National Audubon Society

Page 54-55   Lynwood M. Chace, National Audubon Society; Ewing Galloway, New York

Page 56-57   Hal H. Harrison, National Audubon Society; Elsie M. Rodgers, National Audubon Society

Page 58-59   Soil Conservation Service, U. S. Department of Agriculture; Hugh Spencer, National Audubon Society

Page 60-61   Hal H. Harrison, National Audubon Society; William J. Jahoda, National Audubon Society

Page 62-63   Hal H. Harrison, National Audubon Society; Lynwood M. Chace, National Audubon Society

Page 65   American Museum of Natural History

Page 66-67   Robert C. Hermes, National Audubon Society; Painting by, John James Audubon, National Audubon Society

Page 68-69   Allan D. Cruickshank, National Audubon Society

Page 70-71 Jack Dermid, National Audubon Society

Page 72-73 Donald M. Cooper, National Audubon Society; Allan D. Cruickshank, National Audubon Society

Page 74-75 Allan D. Cruickshank, National Audubon Society; Jack Dermid, National Aud. Soc.

Page 76-77 Allan D. Cruickshank, National Audubon Society; Hugh M. Halliday, National Audubon Society

Page 78-79 Hal H. Harrison, National Audubon Society; John A. Jarosz, Museum of Natural History, University of Minnesota

Page 80-81 Allan D. Cruickshank, National Audubon Society; Don Wooldridge, National Audubon Society

Page 82-83 Hal H. Harrison, National Audubon Society; Roger Tory Peterson, National Audubon Society

Page 85 John H. Gerard, National Audubon Society

Page 86-87 Maslowski & Goodpaster, National Audubon Society; Don Wooldridge, National Audubon Society

Page 88-89 Maslowski & Goodpaster, National Audubon Society; Allan D. Cruickshank, National Audubon Society

Page 90-91 Karl H. Maslowski, National Audubon Society; Standard Oil Company, New Jersey

Page 92-93 Rex Gary Schmidt, Fish and Wildlife Service, U. S. Dept. of Interior; Joe Van Wormer, National Audubon Society

Page 94-95 Joe Van Wormer, National Audubon Society; Hal H. Harrison, National Audubon Society

Page 97 Gerhard Ramberg Painting

Page 98-99 Standard Oil Company, New Jersey

Page 100-101 Soil Conservation Service, U. S. Dept. of Agriculture

Page 102-103 Soil Conservation Service, U. S. Department of Agriculture

Page 104-105 Soil Conservation Service, U. S. Department of Agriculture

Page 106-107 Soil Conservation Service, U. S. Dept. of Agriculture

Page 108-109 Standard Oil Company, New Jersey

Page 110-111 Forest Service, U. S. Department of Agriculture

Page 112-113 Soil Conservation Service, U. S. Department of Agriculture

Page 114-115 Soil Conservation Service, U. S. Department of Agriculture; Don Wooldridge, National Audubon Society

Page 116-117 Missouri Conservation Commission; Oklahoma Extension Service

Page 118-119 Allan D. Cruickshank, National Audubon Society; Hal H. Harrison, National Audubon Society